1st EDITION

Perspectives on Modern World History

The Chinese Cultural Revolution

1st EDITION

Perspectives on Modern World History

The Chinese Cultural Revolution

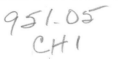

Jeff Hay

Editor

GREENHAVEN PRESS
A part of Gale, Cengage Learning

GALE
CENGAGE Learning·

Detroit • New York • San Francisco • New Haven, Conn • Waterville, Maine • London

Elizabeth Des Chenes, *Managing Editor*

© 2012 Greenhaven Press, a part of Gale, Cengage Learning.

Gale and Greenhaven Press are registered trademarks used herein under license.

For more information, contact:
Greenhaven Press
27500 Drake Rd.
Farmington Hills, MI 48331-3535
Or you can visit our Internet site at gale.cengage.com.

For product information and technology assistance, contact us at
Gale Customer Support, 1-800-877-4253.

For permission to use material from this text or product, submit all requests online at
www.cengage.com/permissions.

Further permissions questions can be e-mailed to permissionrequest@cengage.com.

Articles in Greenhaven Press anthologies are often edited for length to meet page requirements. In addition, original titles of these works are changed to clearly present the main thesis and to explicitly indicate the author's opinion. Every effort is made to ensure that Greenhaven Press accurately reflects the original intent of the authors. Every effort has been made to trace the owners of copyrighted material.

Cover images © Guo Jian She/Redlink/Corbis; © Bettmann/Corbis.

LIBRARY OF CONGRESS CATALOGING-IN-PUBLICATION DATA
The Chinese Cultural Revolution / Jeff Hay, book editor.
p. cm. -- (Perspectives on modern world history)
Includes bibliographical references and index.
ISBN 978-0-7377-5787-3 (hardcover)
1. China--History--Cultural Revolution, 1966–1976. 2. China--History--Cultural Revolution, 1966–1976--Influence. 3. China--History--Cultural Revolution, 1966–1976--Sources. I. Hay, Jeff.
DS778.7.C45627 2012
951.05'6--dc23   2011036227

T 213930

Printed in the United States of America
1 2 3 4 5 6 7 16 15 14 13 12

CONTENTS

atmosphere of chaos and political uncertainty left by the Cultural Revolution in the early 1970s, Mao Zedong's old comrade Deng Xiaoping was brought back into China's inner circle of leadership. Deng had spent 1966 to 1969 isolated and impoverished.

vived the Cultural Revolution. One, Wang Rongfen, wrote a 1966 letter to Mao Zedong opposing the Revolution and suffered greatly for it. Another, Nie Yuangzie, was one of the Revolution's instigators.

CHAPTER 3   Personal Narratives

FOREWORD

"History cannot give us a program for the future, but it can give us a fuller understanding of ourselves, and of our common humanity, so that we can better face the future."
—Robert Penn Warren,
American poet and novelist

The history of each nation is punctuated by momentous events that represent turning points for that nation, with an impact felt far beyond its borders. These events—displaying the full range of human capabilities, from violence, greed, and ignorance to heroism, courage, and strength—are nearly always complicated and multifaceted. Any student of history faces the challenge of grasping the many strands that constitute such world-changing events as wars, social movements, and environmental disasters. But understanding these significant historic events can be enhanced by exposure to a variety of perspectives, whether of people involved intimately or of ones observing from a distance of miles or years. Understanding can also be increased by learning about the controversies surrounding such events and exploring hot-button issues from multiple angles. Finally, true understanding of important historic events involves knowledge of the events' human impact—of the ways such events affected people in their everyday lives—all over the world.

Perspectives on Modern World History examines global historic events from the twentieth-century onward by presenting analysis and observation from numerous vantage points. Each volume offers high school, early college level, and general interest readers a thematically arranged anthology of previously published materials that address a major historical event, with an emphasis on international coverage. Each volume opens with background information on the event, then presents the controversies surrounding that event, and concludes with first-person narratives from people who lived through the event or were affected by it. By providing primary sources from the time of the event, as well as relevant commentary surrounding the event, this series can be used to inform debate, help develop critical thinking skills, increase global awareness, and enhance an understanding of international perspectives on history.

Material in each volume is selected from a diverse range of sources, including journals, magazines, newspapers, nonfiction books, personal narratives, speeches, congressional testimony, government documents, pamphlets, organization newsletters, and position papers. Articles taken from these sources are carefully edited and introduced to provide context and background. Each volume of Perspectives on Modern World History includes an array of views on events of global significance. Much of the material comes from international sources and from US sources that provide extensive international coverage.

Each volume in the Perspectives on Modern World History series also includes:

- A full-color **world map**, offering context and geographic perspective.
- An annotated **table of contents** that provides a brief summary of each essay in the volume.
- An **introduction** specific to the volume topic.
- For each viewpoint, a brief **introduction** that has notes about the author and source of the viewpoint, and that provides a summary of its main points.
- Full-color **charts**, **graphs**, **maps**, and other visual representations.

- Informational **sidebars** that explore the lives of key individuals, give background on historical events, or explain scientific or technical concepts.
- A **glossary** that defines key terms, as needed.
- A **chronology** of important dates preceding, during, and immediately following the event.
- A **bibliography** of additional books, periodicals, and websites for further research.
- A comprehensive **subject index** that offers access to people, places, and events cited in the text.

Perspectives on Modern World History is designed for a broad spectrum of readers who want to learn more about not only history but also current events, political science, government, international relations, and sociology—students doing research for class assignments or debates, teachers and faculty seeking to supplement course materials, and others wanting to improve their understanding of history. Each volume of Perspectives on Modern World History is designed to illuminate a complicated event, to spark debate, and to show the human perspective behind the world's most significant happenings of recent decades.

INTRODUCTION

In the late summer and fall of 1966, tens of thousands of young Chinese people traveled to Beijing, their country's capital. There, for a period of weeks, they gathered in the city's Tiananmen Square, a massive open space frequently used for public meetings and demonstrations. And a few times, during those visits to Tiananmen Square, the assembled young people saw in person the leader they were quickly growing to idolize: chairman of the Chinese Communist Party Mao Zedong. It was the beginning of China's Great Proletarian Cultural Revolution.

The Cultural Revolution, lasting from 1966 to 1976, was the latest in a long series of upheavals in China's nineteenth- and twentieth-century history. During the 1800s, when China was still under the rule of the Qing, or Manchu, Dynasty, large portions of the country fell under the control of Western colonial powers or Japan. When the Qing Dynasty fell in 1911, more than two thousand years of Chinese tradition ended; the Qing Dynasty was the last of a series of dynasties that claimed to rule China with the Mandate of Heaven in combination with legions of officials educated in the philosophy of Confucius. While it was modernizers who helped to overthrow the Qing rulers, and who hoped to learn from the industrialized West, these would-be leaders never managed to establish control over the entire country. Large areas fell instead under the sway of warlords, large landowners rich enough to hire and pay for their own armies. Meanwhile, through the 1920s and 1930s, the Western powers continued to exert a powerful influence over Chinese affairs. The United States, the European powers, and much of the rest of the world recognized as the leader of the nation, Chiang Kai-shek. Chiang led a faction known as the Guomindang that largely continued the process of Westernization but which, again, failed to sway many of the rural warlords who clung to China's centuries-old traditions of hierarchy and order.

Mao Zedong's Chinese Communist Party (CCP) also emerged as a force to be reckoned with in the 1920s. Communist ideology holds forward an ideal of economic as well as political equality among all people, a society in which there would be no hierarchy of social classes. Developed by Europeans such as Karl Marx and Vladimir Lenin in the 1800s and 1900s, Communists believed that this equality would be achieved, first, by overthrowing the rich and powerful in a workers' revolution. Then, over a long period of time, communal ownership of the "means of production"—farms, factories, railroads, ports, mines, and other economic infrastructure—would be achieved, and the state, or the national government, would "wither away." The first attempt at a Communist revolution took place in 1917 in Russia, where participants realized quickly that the transition to a "classless" society seemed to require, at least for the moment, strong state control to educate the masses and to discourage dissent.

The version of communism developed by Mao and his comrades in the CCP differed from that found in Europe. Instead of believing that the roots of communism lay in the industrial working class, Mao argued that the revolution could be begun and carried out by agricultural peasants, as long as they had the proper education and leadership. Either class was made up, Mao claimed, of proletarians, or workers. This viewpoint was necessary, since more than 90 percent of China's people were rural peasants rather than factory workers. Many of them, moreover, were growing resentful of the three forces that seemed to be holding China back: the corruption of Chiang's Guomindang, the oppression of traditional warlords, and the economic exploitation carried out by the Western powers. During the so-called Long March from 1934 to 1936, the Red Army of the CCP escaped the clutches of Chiang's forces, recruited tens of thousands of peasants to their cause, and helped to quash the influence of many warlords.

China's greatest challenge from 1937 to 1945 was a war with Imperial Japan, the same conflict, World War II, that the United States was to enter after a Japanese attack on Hawaii in 1941. Both Chiang's forces and the Red Army, putting aside their differences, fought against a broad Japanese attack and partial occupation that, for all intents and purposes, ended the Western presence in the country. But charges of corruption and inefficiency continued to plague the Guomindang, while the CCP's Red Army fought the invader valiantly. When the Japanese were finally pushed out in 1945, the stage was set for a civil war between the Guomindang and the CCP. This new conflict, and a new phase in China's twentieth-century turmoil, finally ended when the Red Army entered Beijing in 1949 and Chiang's government fled to the island of Taiwan.

China's new regime, with the CCP firmly in control, was known as the People's Republic of China (PRC), as it remains today. At the time of its founding, many Chinese people welcomed at least the hope of stability after decades of revolution, internal upheaval, economic dislocation, and foreign influence. But, they quickly found, the upheavals were to continue. The CCP was always torn apart by internal conflicts among its leaders, including Mao, Lin Biao, Liu Shaoqi, Zhou Enlai, and Deng Xiaoping. These conflicts resulted in shifting policies as to how to move the revolution forward. Mao, as party chairman, exercised the most influence at first. In the mid-1950s his Hundred Flowers Movement promised political openness in hopes of allowing a "hundred flowers" to bloom. But with an increase in political dissent,

Mao quickly declared the effort a failure. Then, from 1958 to 1961, the so-called Great Leap Forward was enacted to speed up industrialization and expand farm production through the establishment of state-owned industries and communal farms. Instead, badly designed policies combined with natural disasters to result in famines that killed millions. By the early 1960s, Mao was losing some of his power in China's inner political circle to economic reformers like Deng Xiaoping. The Great Proletarian Cultural Revolution was Mao's attempt to reestablish himself firmly as China's leading official and cultural figure. A cult of personality, as it happened, had developed around Mao ever since the days of the Long March. It was helped along by his personal charisma and by his ability to make colorful, pithy statements such as those compiled by the People's Liberation Army (PLA; formerly the Red Army) in 1964 as *Quotations from Chairman Mao Tse-tung*. Mao apparently hoped to take advantage of this cult of personality to reinvigorate revolutionary feeling among China's masses.

The chairman's efforts had a ready audience. By the time the CCP announced some of the goals of the Cultural Revolution in 1966, a new generation was beginning to come of age. This generation had grown up since the successful takeover in 1949, and they understood that Mao had been at the center of the effort to end corruption, overbearing traditions, and foreign domination. They also understood, at least vaguely, that the PRC was trying to provide opportunities for ordinary Chinese people that had never existed before. It was members of this generation who packed Tiananmen Square in the late summer and fall of 1966 as their colleges and high schools, almost spontaneously, ended regular coursework in favor of revolutionary activity. The most militant of them had already formed units of what came to be known as Red Guards. Together with Mao, they criticized the "revisionism" of Communists in Soviet Russia and elsewhere. They attacked those who followed the "capitalist road" of free market activity. And they pledged to reject tradition and authority and maintain revolutionary enthusiasm.

The most intense phase of the Cultural Revolution was from 1966 to 1969. At its center were the Red Guards and their continued adoration of Chairman Mao. Carrying their copies of Mao's *Quotations*, Red Guards took over schools and universities and forced teachers to undergo sessions of "self-criticism." They also destroyed temples, museums, and other monuments in order to force a decisive break with China's long history. As units of Red Guards competed with one another to show their devotion to Mao, they performed such gestures as painting entire streets red. The Red Guards' fervor even stretched into the home as children were encouraged to spy on and report their parents for being insufficiently revolutionary. Beatings, sometimes to the point of death, accompanied these rampages. In one of the broader manifestations of the Cultural Revolution, millions of city dwellers were "sent down" to the countryside to live the lives of peasants on communal farms, greatly disrupting everyday life. During these years, China was mostly cut off from the outside world; very few Westerners were able to enter the country at all.

After the chaos of the first years of the Cultural Revolution, the movement began to wind down in the late 1960s and early 1970s. Schools and universities gradually reopened, Red Guards left their activism to take up jobs, and many of those "sent down" returned to their homes and families in the cities. Political uncertainty continued, however. As Mao's grip once again weakened on the inner circles of power, Deng Xiaoping and other reformers returned to influence. Meanwhile, China once again began to reach out to the outside world. In one particularly dramatic moment, US president Richard M. Nixon visited Mao and Chinese premier Zhou Enlai in

1972, improving relations between two countries greatly at odds with one another since 1949.

Mao Zedong died in September 1976. The Cultural Revolution's last gasp was the attempt to maintain power by the so-called Gang of Four, officials who clung to a radical interpretation of communism and wanted to continue elements of the Cultural Revolution. One of the Gang of Four was Jiang Qing, Mao's widow, who had risen to great importance during the Cultural Revolution's most intense years. The Gang's attempt to hold on to the reins of power was thwarted by other politicians and a resurgent, and relatively conservative, People's Liberation Army soon after Mao's death. When Deng Xiaoping officially recognized the end of the Cultural Revolution in 1977, China's many decades of upheaval, uncertainty, and violence seemed finally over.

Since the late 1970s, China has grown to be one of the world's largest economies and, by the reckoning of many experts, a potential twenty-first-century superpower. Although episodes of crisis have continued—most notably the crackdown of pro-democracy student demonstrators in Tiananmen Square in 1989—China's political and social worlds have remained relatively stable compared to the chaotic first eight decades of the twentieth century. Meanwhile, and in contrast to the goals of the Cultural Revolution and in the context of a "lost generation" of former Red Guards, China has apparently prospered by taking, as Chairman Mao derisively phrased it, the "capitalist road." For his part, and perhaps surprisingly, Mao Zedong himself remains at the center of a cult of personality even into the twenty-first century.

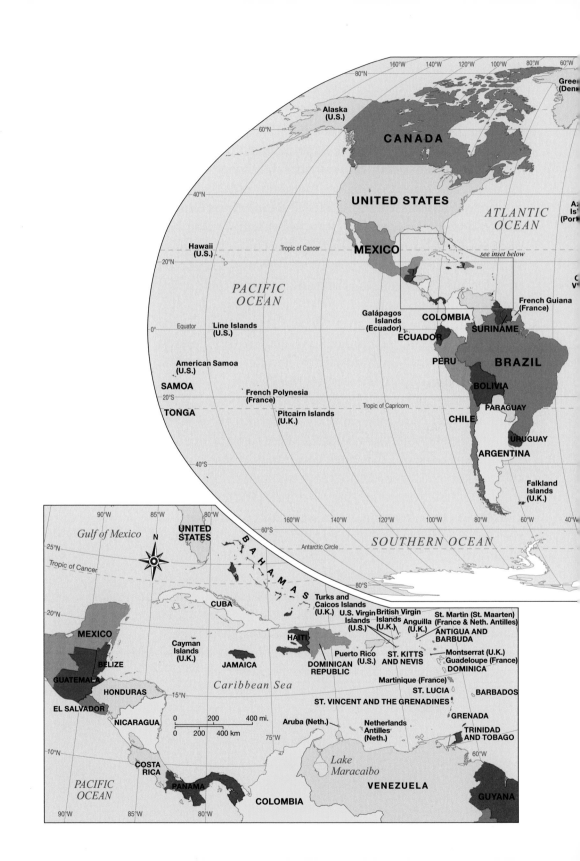

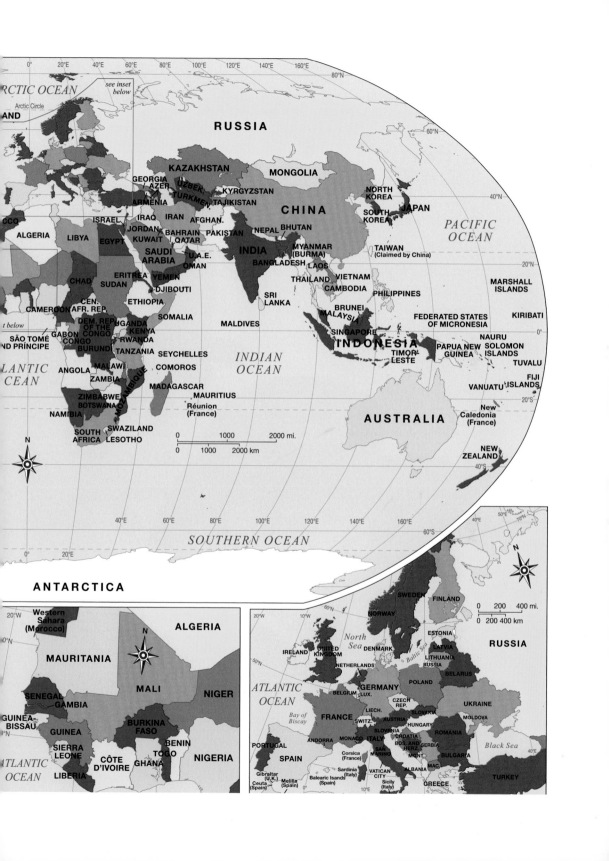

CHAPTER 1

Historical Background on the Chinese Cultural Revolution

The Chinese Cultural Revolution: An Overview

Junhao Hong

The Chinese Cultural Revolution lasted from 1966 to 1976. In the following selection, a scholar provides an overview of the event. He notes that the Revolution intended to instill in China's people, especially its younger generations, a sense of an ongoing transformation of not only society but of the understanding of history. Leaders encouraged the formation of units of so-called Red Guards, mostly made up of younger people, to criticize old ways and old habits of thought; these units sometimes also engaged in "revolutionary" violence. The Cultural Revolution came to require very strict governmental control of books and of the media. During the most intense, early years of the Cultural Revolution, from 1966 to 1969, China was even closed off to the outside world. Political upheavals slowly unwound the revolution, and the death of Chinese leader Mao Zedong in 1976 finally brought a formal end to what the author

Photo on previous page: The *Little Red Book*, containing Mao Zedong's teachings, was the basic text of the Cultural Revolution. (**Rolls Press/Popperfoto/Getty Images.**)

SOURCE. Junhao Hong, "Chinese Cultural Revolution," *Encyclopedia of Political Communication.* Thousand Oaks, CA: Sage Publications, Inc., 2008, pp. 100–101. Copyright © 2008 by Sage Publications, Inc. All rights reserved. Reproduced by permission.

characterizes as a "disaster" for China. Junhao Hong is an assistant professor of communication at the State University of New York, Buffalo.

The Chinese Cultural Revolution started in October 1966 and ended in October 1976. It was launched by Mao Zedong, the late chairman and the founder of the Chinese Communist Party, during his last decade in power in an attempt to renew the spirit of the Chinese revolution. It began as a civil war of sorts—a war of slogans, ideology, and ideas, but later it became almost a nationwide military conflict among different "revolutionary units" of workers, peasants, and college students. The purpose of the Cultural Revolution, as Mao claimed, was to guarantee China would never change its "Marxist color," and in order to achieve this goal Mao said that China had to engage in class struggle at all levels, in all aspects, for all times, and the Cultural Revolution was the new format of class struggle in China's new historical stage.

Breaking the Four Olds

Unfortunately, the Cultural Revolution was, in fact, a distorted and atypical phase of political extremism and forced mobilization. It was not only iconoclastic but also barbaric in its efforts to destroy Chinese culture. The Maoist slogan *po si jiu*—meaning break the four olds: old ideas, old customs, old culture, and old habits— was used by hundreds of millions of people to destroy the "old world" in order to establish a "new world." Virtually speaking, the Cultural Revolution was a mixture of a power struggle among party leaders, an ideological campaign for Mao's revolutionary ideas, and a massive

> Mao closed all schools and called students to join Red Guard units.

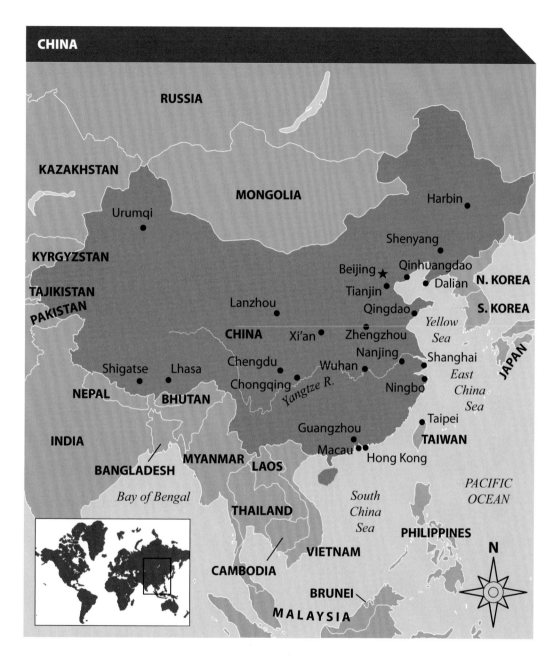

"re-education" movement of every person in China. When the Cultural Revolution started, Mao closed all schools and called students to join Red Guard units. Millions of the young Red Guards were used for criticism of party officials, intellectuals, and anything that was perceived to contain "bourgeois [capitalist, middle-class] values." The Red Guards became a "shock force" and began to "bombard" both the regular party headquarters in Beijing and those at the regional and provincial levels across the whole nation. The "four big rights"—speaking out freely, airing views fully, holding great debates, and writing big-character posters—became the revolutionary weapon of Mao's youthful followers to criticize all kinds of "class enemies."

The effects of the Cultural Revolution directly or indirectly touched essentially all of China's populace. During the Cultural Revolution, much economic activity was halted, with revolution being the primary objective of many. But the Cultural Revolution mostly affected and changed the realms of culture, education, ideology, and

Workers at a steel plant read heavily censored newspapers in 1969. (AP Photo.)

communication and media. Mao long believed that although the bourgeoisie had been overthrown, it was still trying to use the old ideas, culture, customs, and habits of exploiting classes to corrupt the masses, capture their minds, and endeavor to stage a comeback; therefore, the proletariat must do just the opposite: it must meet head-on every challenge of the bourgeoisie especially in the ideological field. Consequently, the media was a key battleground of ideology and became a particularly important site of class struggle. One of the first moves Mao and his allies made was to gain control over the propaganda apparatus. Media was used to safeguard the directions of the Cultural Revolution and to give its partisans powerful psychological and political support. All communication means and media outlets were exclusively used to propagate an ultraleftist ideology and mass culture, and all of the media's functions became a single one, that is, to publicize, explain, and express the theory and practice of "class struggle."

Cultural Restrictions

For most of the years during the Cultural Revolution, people were forbidden to read anything except Mao's *Little Red Book*, a book of the excerpts from Mao's works that propagate both the Marxist doctrine and Mao's revolutionary theory. Feudalistic, fascist, journalistic control reached its climax. Anyone who expressed ideas even minimally different from Mao's was condemned as a "class enemy." Every editorial, critique, commentary, and signed article is written according to the desires of the power holders. Moreover, when writing their articles, some journalists just copied Central Party Committee or Provincial Party Committee documents, or the speeches of their leaders, because it

> Anyone who expressed ideas even minimally different from Mao's was condemned as a 'class enemy.'

was politically safe to copy the Central Party Committee inspected important manuscripts at the *People's Daily*—the mouthpiece of Mao and his allies—and to copy the Provincial Party Committee-inspected provincial newspaper articles. The press thus became a thousand newspapers with one face. Many broadcasters were dismissed—some were sent to factories to do physical labor, some moved to the countryside to receive "reeducation" by peasants, and others stayed in radio and television stations to criticize themselves for being bourgeois-influenced and to prepare for new "people's broadcasting stations." The broadcasting media's newscasts were nothing but what the *People's Daily* reported. Television entertainment programming was reduced to a minimum and consisted exclusively of ideological content. All feature film production was closed down from 1966 to 1970, and all but a handful of the movies made in China in the previous 17 years between 1949 and 1966 were banned. Many older artists suffered imprisonment, violence, and physical deprivation. During the whole Cultural Revolution, the only films made were of the "model performances" endorsed by the party's new cultural leaders.

To the outside world, China was implementing Mao's anti-imperialism, antirevisionism, and anticapitalism principles. There were very few foreign programs on television and cinema screens. Importing media and cultural products from foreign countries—imperialist countries such as the United States, revisionist countries such as the former Soviet Union, and capitalist countries such as Japan and Britain—were thought only to poison the Chinese people, change China's socialist color, and destroy the communist ideology. Thus, the importation of foreign television programming and film was almost at zero. Although foreign contacts were gradually reestablished after 1969, and this situation improved to a large extent when [US] President [Richard] Nixon visited China in 1972, large-scale, major changes in television program importation were not seen until China entered the reform era after 1978.

Fortunately, in October, 1976, just less than a month after Mao's death on September 9, Mao's wife Jiang Qing and her three principal associates, Wang Hongwen, Zhang Chunqiao, and Yao Wenyuan—denounced as the Gang of Four—were arrested by Hua Guofeng, the Mao-appointed successor, with the assistance of two senior political bureau members, Minister of National Defense Ye Jianying and Wang Dongxing, which symbolized the end of the Cultural Revolution. Today, the Cultural Revolution is seen by most people inside and outside of China, including the Communist Party of China and Chinese democracy movement supporters, as an unmitigated disaster, the bloodiest and darkest period in contemporary Chinese history and an event to be avoided in the future.

China's Leaders Proclaim the Goals and Tactics of the Cultural Revolution

Central Committee of the Chinese Communist Party

The following selection is taken from an official statement made by the ruling Central Committee of the Chinese Communist Party in 1966 that marks the beginning of the Cultural Revolution. In it, leaders describe their overall purpose, desirable tactics, and dangers to watch out for using sixteen points. Inherent in all of them is a call for loyalty to and dedication to the guidance provided by Communist Party chairman Mao Zedong. Chinese Communists had succeeded in taking over their nation in 1949. In basic terms, Communists wanted to end the social control of the bourgeoisie, by which they meant capitalists and industrialists, and create a society oriented around the proletariat, or working classes. In the sixteen points, leaders acknowledge that the bourgeoisie was overthrown but that the revolution was not yet complete; too many people, including persons of influence, were still taking the "capitalist road." A transformation of ideas and of education was now necessary.

SOURCE. Central Committee of the Chinese Communist Party, "Decision Concerning the Great Proletarian Cultural Revolution," August 8, 1966, pp. 430–440.

1. A New Stage in the Socialist Revolution

The Great Proletarian Cultural Revolution now unfolding is a great revolution that touches people to their very souls and constitutes a new stage in the development of the socialist revolution in our country, a stage which is both broader and deeper.

At the Tenth Plenary Session of the Eighth Central Committee of the Party, Comrade Mao Tse-tung [also spelled "Zedong"] said: to overthrow a political power, it is always necessary first of all to create public opinion, to do work in the ideological sphere. This is true for the revolutionary class as well as for the counter-revolutionary class. This thesis of Comrade Mao Tse-tung's has been proved entirely correct in practice.

Although the bourgeoisie [the capitalist ruling class] has been overthrown, it is still trying to use the old ideas, culture, customs and habits of the exploiting classes to corrupt the masses, capture their minds and endeavour to stage a comeback. The proletariat [working classes] must do the exact opposite: it must meet head-on every challenge of the bourgeoisie in the ideological field and use the new ideas, culture, customs and habits of the proletariat to change the mental outlook of the whole of society. At present, our objective is to struggle against and overthrow those persons in authority who are taking the capitalist road, to criticize and repudiate the reactionary bourgeois academic 'authorities' and the ideology of the bourgeoisie and all other exploiting classes and to transform education, literature and art and all other parts of the superstructure not in correspondence with the socialist economic base, so as to facilitate the consolidation and development of the socialist system.

> " Our objective is to struggle against and overthrow those persons in authority who are taking the capitalist road. "

2. The Main Current and the Twists and Turns

The masses of the workers, peasants, soldiers, revolutionary intellectuals, and revolutionary cadres [officials] form the main force in this Great Cultural Revolution. Large numbers of revolutionary young people, previously unknown, have become courageous and daring pathbreakers. They are vigorous in action and intelligent. Through the media of big-character posters and great debates, they argue things out, expose and criticize thoroughly, and launch resolute attacks on the open and hidden representatives of the bourgeoisie. In such a great revolutionary movement, it is hardly avoidable that they should show shortcomings of one kind or another;

Posters with Mao's thoughts and Communist Party propaganda completely cover a building in Canton in 1966. (**Richard Harrington/Three Lions/ Getty Images.**)

The Great Leap Forward

One reason why Chairman Mao Zedong called for a Great Proletarian Cultural Revolution in 1966 was that he feared his political influence was waning. He had been criticized since the early 1960s because of the effects of a misconceived economic initiative known as the Great Leap Forward.

The Great Leap Forward lasted from 1958 to 1961. Mao intended it to allow for China to engage in a rapid industrial advance and, at the same time, spur agricultural production. Major changes were planned for both the industrial and agricultural sectors of the economy. In accordance with Communist ideas, hundreds of state-run factories were established and thousands of former farmers became factory workers. A related measure that drew peasants away from growing food was Mao's encouragement of small-scale steel production in rural areas, even in the backyards of houses. The steel that resulted was often of very poor quality, yet Mao valued the effort anyway because he thought it inspired revolutionary feelings.

In agriculture, private farms were abolished and replaced by state-run communes. In addition, state authorities tried to introduce unproven farming technologies, such as new seed strains, in hopes of increasing yields. The negative effects of these measures were widespread. Peasants were uprooted from centuries-old traditions, and now relied on the state for their livelihood. They also faced constant nagging and threats from Communist cadres, or officials, who in their turn were prone to lie about production amounts to impress their superiors. Meanwhile, the new technologies often proved ineffective, resulting in declines in production rather than increases.

Declining farm yields, a lack of labor to harvest crops, and poor distribution of food combined with natural disasters such as droughts and floods to produce the worst effect of the Great Leap Forward: famine. Estimates vary widely, but at least ten million people died as a result of Mao's attempt to force this rapid economic transformation.

Although he remained the chairman of the Communist Party of China, Mao stepped aside as an active leader in Chinese politics during latter stages of the Great Leap Forward, understanding that he would be blamed for its ineffectiveness and tragic consequences. Economic policy was then placed in the hands of reformers like Deng Xiaoping and Liu Shaoqi, who favored more openness and less state control. When Mao, in 1966, tried to reassert himself with the Cultural Revolution, both Deng and Liu were accused of "taking the capitalist road" and, for a time, banished from the inner circles of Chinese politics.

however, their general revolutionary orientation has been correct from the beginning. This is the main current in the Great Proletarian Cultural Revolution. It is the general direction along which this revolution continues to advance.

Since the Cultural Revolution is a revolution, it inevitably meets with resistance. This resistance comes chiefly from those in authority who have wormed their way into the Party and are taking the capitalist road. It also comes from the force of habits from the old society. At present, this resistance is still fairly strong and stubborn. But after all, the Great Proletarian Cultural Revolution is an irresistible general trend. There is abundant evidence that such resistance will be quickly broken down once the masses become fully aroused.

Because the resistance is fairly strong, there will be reversals and even repeated reversals in this struggle. There is no harm in this. It tempers the proletariat and other working people, and especially the younger generation, teaches them lessons and gives them experience, and helps them to understand that the revolutionary road zigzags and does not run smoothly.

3. Put Daring Above Everything Else and Boldly Arouse the Masses

The outcome of this Great Cultural Revolution will be determined by whether or not the Party leadership dares boldly to arouse the masses.

Currently, there are four different situations with regard to the leadership being given to the movement of Cultural Revolution by Party organizations at various levels:

1. There is the situation in which the persons in charge of Party organizations stand in the van of the movement and dare to arouse the masses boldly. They put daring above everything else, they are dauntless com-

munist fighters and good pupils of Chairman Mao. They advocate the big-character posters and great debates. They encourage the masses to expose every kind of ghost and monster and also to criticize the shortcomings and errors in the work of the persons in charge. This correct kind of leadership is the result of putting proletarian politics in the forefront and Mao Tse-tung's thought in the lead.

2. In many units, the persons in charge have a very poor understanding of the task of leadership in this great struggle, their leadership is far from being conscientious and effective, and they accordingly find themselves incompetent and in a weak position. They put fear above everything else, stick to outmoded ways and regulations, and are unwilling to break away from conventional practices and move ahead. They have been taken unaware by the new order of things, the revolutionary order of the masses, with the result that their leadership lags behind the situation, lags behind the masses.

3. In some units, the persons in charge, who made mistakes of one kind or another in the past, are even more prone to put fear above everything else, being afraid that the masses will catch them out. Actually, if they make serious self-criticism and accept the criticism of the masses, the Party and the masses will make allowances for their mistakes. But if the persons in charge don't, they will continue to make mistakes and become obstacles to the mass movement.

4. Some units are controlled by those who have wormed their way into the Party and are taking the capitalist road. Such persons in authority are extremely afraid of being exposed by the masses and therefore seek every possible pretext to suppress the mass movement. They resort to such tactics as shifting the targets for attack and turning black into white in

an attempt to lead the movement astray. When they find themselves very isolated and no longer able to carry on as before, they resort still more to intrigues, stabbing people in the back, spreading rumours, and blurring the distinction between revolution and counter-revolution as much as they can, all for the purpose of attacking the revolutionaries.

What the Central Committee of the Party demands of the Party committees at all levels is that they persevere in giving correct leadership, put daring above everything else, boldly arouse the masses, change the state of weakness and incompetence where it exists, encourage those comrades who have made mistakes but are willing to correct them to cast off their mental burdens and join in the struggle, and dismiss from their leading posts all those in authority who are taking the capitalist road and so make possible to recapture of the leadership for the proletarian revolution.

> Trust the masses, rely on them and respect their initiative.

4. Let the Masses Educate Themselves in the Movement

In the Great Proletarian Cultural Revolution, the only method is for the masses to liberate themselves, and any method of doing things in their stead must not be used.

Trust the masses, rely on them and respect their initiative. Cast out fear. Don't be afraid of disturbances. Chairman Mao has often told us that revolution cannot be so very refined, so gentle, so temperate, kind, courteous, restrained and magnanimous. Let the masses educate themselves in this great revolutionary movement and learn to distinguish between right and wrong and between correct and incorrect ways of doing things.

Make the fullest use of big-character posters and great debates to argue matters out, so that the masses can clarify the correct views, criticize the wrong views and expose all the ghosts and monsters. In this way the masses will be able to raise their political consciousness in the course of the struggle, enhance their abilities and talents, distinguish right from wrong and draw a clear line between ourselves and the enemy.

5. Firmly Apply the Class Line of the Party

Who are our enemies? Who are our friends? This is a question of the first importance for the revolution and it is likewise a question of the first importance for the Great Cultural Revolution.

Party leadership should be good at discovering the left and developing and strengthening the ranks of the left; it should firmly rely on the revolutionary left. During the movement this is the only way to isolate the most reactionary rightists thoroughly, win over the middle and unite with the great majority so that by the end of the movement we shall achieve the unity of more than 95 per cent of the cadres and more than 95 per cent of the masses.

Concentrate all forces to strike at the handful of ultra-reactionary bourgeois rightists and counter-revolutionary revisionists, and expose and criticize to the full their crimes against the Party, against socialism and against Mao Tse-tung's thought so as to isolate them to the maximum.

The main target of the present movement is those within the Party who are in authority and are taking the capitalist road. . . .

6. Correctly Handle Contradictions Among the People

A strict distinction must be made between the two different types of contradictions: those among the people and those between ourselves and the enemy. Contradictions among the people must not be made into contradictions between ourselves and the enemy; nor must contradictions between ourselves and the enemy be regarded as contradictions among the people.

It is normal for the masses to hold different views. Contention between different views is unavoidable, necessary and beneficial. In the course of normal and full debate, the masses will affirm what is right, correct what is wrong and gradually reach unanimity. . . .

7. Be on Guard Against Those Who Brand the Revolutionary Masses as "Counter-Revolutionaries"

In certain schools, units, and work teams of the Cultural Revolution, some of the persons in charge have organized counter-attacks against the masses who put up big-character posters criticizing them. These people have even advanced such slogans as: opposition to the leaders of a unit or a work team means opposition to the Central Committee of the Party, means opposition to the Party and socialism, means counter-revolution. In this way it is inevitable that their blows will fall on some really revolutionary activists.

This is an error on matters of orientation, an error of line, and is absolutely impermissible.

A number of persons who suffer from serious ideological errors, and particularly some of the anti-Party and anti-socialist rightists, are taking advantage of certain shortcomings and mistakes in the mass movement to spread rumours and gossip, and engage in agitation, deliberately branding some of the masses as 'counter-revolutionaries'. It is necessary to beware of such 'pickpockets' and expose their tricks in good time.

In the course of the movement, with the exception of cases of active counter-revolutionaries where there is clear evidence of crimes such as murder, arson, poisoning, sabotage or theft of state secrets, which should be handled in accordance with the law, no measures should be taken against students at universities, colleges, middle schools and primary schools because of problems that arise in the movement.

To prevent the struggle from being diverted from its main target, it is not allowed, under whatever pretext, to incite the masses or the students to struggle against each other. Even proven rightists should be dealt with on the merits of each case at a later stage of the movement.

8. The Question of Cadres

The cadres fall roughly into the following four categories:

1. good;

2. comparatively good;

3. those who have made serious mistakes but have not become anti-Party, anti-socialist rightists;

4. the small number of anti-Party, anti-socialist rightists.

In ordinary situations, the first two categories (good and comparatively good) are the great majority.

The anti-Party, anti-socialist rightists must be fully exposed, refuted, overthrown and completely discredited and their influence eliminated. At the same time, they should be given a chance to turn over a new leaf.

9. Cultural Revolutionary Groups, Committees and Congresses

Many new things have begun to emerge in the Great Proletarian Cultural Revolution. The Cultural Revolutionary groups, committees and other organizational forms created by the masses in many schools and units are something new and of great historic importance.

These Cultural Revolutionary groups, committees and congresses are excellent new forms of organization whereby the masses educate themselves under the leadership of the Communist Party. They are an excellent bridge to keep our Party in close contact with the masses. They are organs of power of the proletarian Cultural Revolution.

The struggle of the proletariat against the old ideas, culture, customs and habits left over by all the exploiting classes over thousands of years will necessarily take a very, very long time. Therefore, the Cultural Revolutionary groups, committees and congresses should not be temporary organizations but permanent, standing mass organizations. They are suitable not only for colleges, schools and government and other organizations, but generally also for factories, mines, other enterprises, urban districts and villages. . . .

10. Educational Reform

In the Great Proletarian Cultural Revolution a most important task is to transform the old educational system and the old principles and methods of teaching.

In this Great Cultural Revolution, the phenomenon of our schools being dominated by bourgeois intellectuals must be completely changed.

In every kind of school we must apply thoroughly the policy advanced by Comrade Mao Tse-tung of education serving proletarian politics and education being combined with productive labour, so as to enable those receiving an education to develop morally, intellectually and physically and to become labourers with socialist consciousness and culture.

> The period of schooling should be shortened. Courses should be fewer and better.

The period of schooling should be shortened. Courses should be fewer and better. The teaching material should be thoroughly transformed, in some cases beginning with simplifying complicated material. While their main task is to study, students should also learn other things. That is to say, in addition to their studies they should also learn industrial work, farming and military affairs, and take part in the struggles of the Cultural Revolution to criticize the bourgeoisie as these struggles occur.

11. The Question of Criticizing by Name in the Press

In the course of the mass movement of the Cultural Revolution, the criticism of bourgeois and feudal ideology should be well combined with the dissemination of the proletarian world outlook and of Marxism-Leninism, Mao Tse-tung's thought.

Criticism should be organized of typical bourgeois representatives who have wormed their way into the Party and typical reactionary bourgeois academic 'authorities', and this should include criticism of various kinds of reactionary views in philosophy, history, political economy and education, in works and theories of literature and art, in theories of natural science, and in other fields.

Criticism of anyone by name in the press should be decided after discussion by the Party committee at the same level, and in some cases submitted to the Party committee at a higher level for approval.

12. Policy Towards Scientists, Technicians and Ordinary Members of Working Staffs

As regards scientists, technicians and ordinary members of working staffs, as long as they are patriotic, work energetically, are not against the Party and socialism, and maintain no illicit relations with any foreign country, we should in the present movement continue to apply the policy of 'unity, criticism, unity'. Special care should be taken of those scientists and scientific and technical personnel who have made contributions. Efforts should be made to help them gradually transform their world outlook and their style of work.

13. The Question of Arrangements for Integration with the Socialist Education Movement in City and Countryside

The cultural and educational units and leading organs of the Party and government in the large and medium cities are the points of concentration of the present proletarian Cultural Revolution.

The Great Cultural Revolution has enriched the socialist education movement in both city and countryside and raised it to a higher level. Efforts should be made to conduct these two movements in close combination. Arrangements to this effect may be made by various regions and departments in the light of the specific conditions.

The socialist education movement now going on in the countryside and in enterprises in the cities should not be upset where the original arrangements are appropriate and the movement is going well, but should continue in accordance with the original arrangements. However, the questions that are arising in the present Great Proletarian Cultural Revolution should be put to the masses for discussion at the proper time, so as to further foster vigorously proletarian ideology and eradicate bourgeois ideology.

In some places, the Great Proletarian Cultural Revolution is being used as the focus in order to add momentum to the socialist education movement and clean things up in the fields of politics, ideology, organization and economy. This may be done where the local Party committee thinks it appropriate.

14. Take Firm Hold of the Revolution and Stimulate Production

The aim of the Great Proletarian Cultural Revolution is to revolutionize people's ideology and as a consequence to achieve greater, faster, better and more economical results in all fields of work. If the masses are fully aroused and proper arrangements are made, it is possible to carry on both the Cultural Revolution and production without one hampering the other, while guaranteeing high quality in all our work.

The Great Proletarian Cultural Revolution is a powerful motive force for the development of the social productive forces in our country. Any idea of counterposing the Great Cultural Revolution to the development of production is incorrect.

15. The Armed Forces

In the armed forces, the cultural revolution and the socialist education movement should be carried out in accordance with the instructions of the Military Commission of the Central Committee of the Party and the General Political Department of the People's Liberation Army.

16. Mao Tse-Tung's Thought Is the Guide to Action in the Great Proletarian Cultural Revolution

In the Great Proletarian Cultural Revolution, it is imperative to hold aloft the great red banner of Mao Tse-tung's thought and put proletarian politics in command. The movement for the creative study and application of Chairman Mao Tse-tung's works should be carried forward among the masses of the workers, peasants and soldiers, the cadres and the intellectuals, and Mao Tse-tung's thought should be taken as the guide to action in the Cultural Revolution. . . .

> Party committees at all levels must abide by the directions given by Chairman Mao over the years.

Party committees at all levels must abide by the directions given by Chairman Mao over the years, namely that they should thoroughly apply the mass line of 'from the masses, to the masses' and that they should be pupils before they become teachers. They should try to avoid being one-sided or narrow. They should foster materialist dialectics and oppose metaphysics and scholasticism.

The Great Proletarian Cultural Revolution is bound to achieve brilliant victory under the leadership of the Central Committee of the Party headed by Comrade Mao Tse-tung.

The Main Purpose of the Cultural Revolution Is to Sweep Away Old Ideas

Jiefangjun Bao

The following viewpoint was originally published in the *People's Liberation Army Daily*, a state-run Chinese newspaper, in 1966 at the onset of the Cultural Revolution. In the article, the author clearly identifies the main weapon of the Revolution: the writings and statements of Mao Zedong (also spelled "Tse-tung"), the Chinese leader and Communist Party chairman. "Mao Zedong Thought" was to provide all necessary guidance and answers to those carrying out China's continued transformation. By concentrating on Mao Zedong's thought, the author notes, the Chinese people will be fully able to understand and to deal with certain dangers. These included the United States and its "imperialist" ideology, as well as the "revisionism" of Communist ideals then taking hold in the Soviet Union, the world's other large Communist power. Chinese leaders quickly assembled a collection of Mao Zedong's thought

---

SOURCE. Jiefangjun Bao, "Mao Tse-Tung's Thought Is the Telescope and Microscope of Our Revolutionary Cause," *Peking Review*, no. 24, June 10, 1966. Copyright © 1966 by Jiefangjun Bao. All rights reserved. Reproduced by permission.

known commonly as the *Little Red Book*, and it became the basic text of the Cultural Revolution.

The current great socialist cultural revolution is a great revolution to sweep away all monsters and a great revolution that remoulds the ideology of people and touches their souls. What weapon should be used to sweep away all monsters? What ideology should be applied to arm people's minds and remould their souls? The most powerful ideological weapon, the only one, is the great Mao Tse-tung's thought.

Mao Tse-tung's thought is our political orientation, the highest instruction for our actions; it is our ideological and political telescope and microscope for observing and analysing all things. In this unprecedented great cultural revolution, we should apply Mao Tse-tung's thought to observe, analyse and transform everything, and, in a word, put it in command of everything. We should apply Mao Tse-tung's thought to attack boldly and seize victory.

> Our struggle against the anti-Party, anti-socialist black line and gangsters is a mighty, life-and-death class struggle.

Chairman Mao teaches us: "After the enemies with guns have been wiped out, there will still be enemies without guns; they are bound to struggle desperately against us; we must never regard these enemies lightly." Our struggle against the anti-Party, anti-socialist black line and gangsters is a mighty, life-and-death class struggle. The enemies without guns are more hidden, cunning, sinister and vicious than the enemies with guns. The representatives of the [capitalist] bourgeoisie and all monsters, including the modern revisionists [those who want to modify Communist ideology], often oppose the red flag by hoisting a red flag and oppose Marxism-Leninism and Mao Tse-tung's thought under the cloak of Marxism-Leninism and Mao Tse-tung's thought when they attack the Party and socialism, because Marxism-Leninism and Mao Tse-tung's thought are becoming more popular day by day, the prestige of our Party and Chairman Mao are incomparably high and the dictatorship of the proletariat [working class] of our country is becoming more consolidated. These are the tactics that the revisionists always use in opposing Marxism-Leninism. This is a new characteristic of the class struggle under the conditions of the dictatorship of the proletariat.

Enemies of the Revolution

The many facts exposed during the great cultural revolution show us more clearly that the anti-Party and anti-socialist elements are all careerists, schemers and hypocrites of the exploiting classes. They are double-dealing. They feign compliance while acting in opposition. They appear to be men but are demons at heart. They speak human language to your face, but talk devil's language behind your back. They are wolves in sheep's clothing and man-eating tigers with smiling faces. They often use the phrases of Marxism-Leninism and Mao Tse-tung's thought as a cover while greatly publicizing diametrically opposed views behind the word "but" and smuggling in bourgeois and revisionist stuff. The enemies holding a false red banner are ten times more vicious than enemies holding a white banner. Wolves in sheep's clothing are ten times more sinister than ordinary wolves. Tigers with smiling faces are ten times more ferocious than tigers with their fangs bared and their claws sticking out. Sugar-coated bullets are ten times more destructive than real bullets. A fortress is most vulnerable when attacked from within. Enemies who have wormed their way into our ranks are far more dangerous than enemies operating in the open. We must give this serious attention and be highly vigilant.

In such a very complicated and acute class struggle, how are we to draw a clear-cut line between the enemy and ourselves and maintain a firm stand? How are we to distinguish between revolutionaries and counter-revolutionaries, genuine revolutionaries and sham revolutionaries, and Marxism-Leninism and revisionism? We must master Mao Tse-tung's thought, the powerful ideological weapon, and use it as a telescope and a microscope to observe all matters. With the invincible Mao Tse-tung's thought, with the scientific world outlook and methodology of dialectical materialism and historical materialism which have been developed by Chairman Mao, and with the sharp weapon of Chairman Mao's theory of classes and class struggle, we have the highest criterion for judging right and wrong. We are able to penetrate deeply into all things and to recognize the whole through observation of the part. We can see the essence behind outward appearance, and clear away the miasma to achieve profound insight into things and thus monsters of all sorts will be unable to hide themselves. We can stand on an eminence, become far-sighted and view the whole situation, the future and the great significance and far-reaching influence of the great socialist cultural revolution. We can advance without the slightest fear and stand in the forefront of the great socialist cultural revolution.

Workers Need to Hold Firm

Chairman Mao teaches us: "The proletariat seeks to transform the world according to its own world outlook, so does the bourgeoisie." In the sharp clash between the two world outlooks, either you crush me, or I crush you. It will not do to sit on the fence; there is no middle road. The overthrown bourgeoisie, in their plots for restoration and subversion, always give first place to ideology, take hold of ideology and the superstructure. The representatives of the bourgeoisie, by using their position

and power, usurped and controlled the leadership of a number of departments, did all they could to spread bourgeois and revisionist poison through the media of literature, the theatre, films, music, the arts, the press, periodicals, the radio, publications and academic research and in schools, etc., in an attempt to corrupt people's minds and perpetrate "peaceful evolution" as ideological preparation and preparation of public opinion for capitalist restoration. If our proletarian ideology does not take over the position, then the bourgeois ideology will have free rein; it will gradually nibble away and chew you up bit by bit. Once proletarian ideology gives way, so will the superstructure and the economic base and this means the restoration of capitalism. Therefore, we must arm our minds with Mao Tse-tung's thought and establish a firm proletarian world outlook. We must use the great Mao Tse-tung's thought to fight and completely destroy the bourgeois ideological and cultural positions.

Workers, like these young medics at a Beijing Hospital reading the *Little Red Book*, were required to study Chairman Mao's works. (AFP/Getty Images.)

Mao Tse-tung's thought is the acme of Marxism-Leninism in the present era. It is living Marxism-Leninism at its highest. It is the powerful, invincible weapon of the Chinese people, and it is also a powerful, invincible weapon of the revolutionary people the world over. Mao Tse-tung's thought has proved to be invincible truth through the practice of China's democratic revolution, socialist revolution and socialist construction, and through the struggle in the international sphere against U.S. imperialism and its lackeys and against Khrushchev [the Soviet Union's] revisionism. Chairman Mao has, with the gifts of genius, creatively and comprehensively developed Marxism-Leninism. Basing himself on the fundamental theses of Marxism-Leninism, Chairman Mao has summed up the experience of the practice of the Chinese revolution and the world revolution, and the painful lesson of the usurpation of the leadership of the Party and the state of the Soviet Union by the modern revisionist clique, systematically put forward the theory concerning classes, class contradictions and class struggle that exist in socialist society, greatly enriched and developed the Marxist-Leninist theory on the dictatorship of the proletariat, and put forward a series of wise policies aimed at opposing and preventing revisionism and the restoration of capitalism. All this ensures that our country will always maintain its revolutionary spirit and never change its colour, and it is of extremely great theoretical and practical significance to the revolutionary cause of the international proletariat. Every sentence by Chairman Mao is truth, and carries more weight than ten thousand ordinary sentences. As the Chinese people master Mao Tse-tung's thought, China will be prosperous and ever-victorious. Once the world's people master Mao Tse-

> Every sentence by Chairman Mao is truth, and carries more weight than ten thousand ordinary sentences.

tung's thought which is living Marxism-Leninism, they are sure to win their emancipation, bury imperialism, modern revisionism and all reactionaries lock, stock and barrel, and realize communism throughout the world step by step.

The Purpose of the Cultural Revolution

The most fundamental task in the great socialist cultural revolution in our country is to eliminate thoroughly the old ideology and culture, the old customs and habits which were fostered by all the exploiting classes for thousands of years to poison the minds of the people, and to create and form an entirely new, proletarian ideology and culture, new customs and habits among the masses of the people. This is to creatively study and apply Mao Tse-tung's thought in tempestuous class struggle, popularize it and let it become closely integrated with the masses of workers, peasants and soldiers. Once the masses grasp it, Mao Tse-tung's thought will be transformed into a mighty material force. Facts show that those armed with Mao Tse-tung's thought are the bravest, wisest, most united, most steadfast in class stand and have the sharpest sight. In this great, stormy cultural revolution, the masses of workers, peasants and soldiers are the main force—this is the result of their efforts in creatively studying and applying Mao Tse-tung's thought and arming their ideology with it. This is another eloquent proof of the fact that when the masses of workers, peasants and soldiers master the political telescope and microscope of Mao Tse-tung's thought, they are invincible and ever-triumphant. None of the monsters can escape their sharp sight, no matter what the tricks used or what the clever camouflage employed, "36 stratagems" or "72 metamorphoses." Not a single bourgeois stronghold can escape thorough destruction.

The attitude towards Mao Tse-tung's thought, whether to accept it or resist it, to support it or oppose it, to love it warmly or be hostile to it, this is the touch-stone to test and the watershed between true revolution and sham revolution, between revolution and counter-revolution, between Marxism-Leninism and revision-ism. He who wants to make revolution must accept Mao Tse-tung's thought and act in accordance with it. A counter-revolutionary will inevitably disparage, distort, resist, attack and oppose Mao Tse-tung's thought. The "authorities" of the bourgeoisie and all monsters, includ-ing the modern revisionists, use every means to slander Mao Tse-tung's thought, and they are extremely hostile to the creative study and application of Mao Tse-tung's works by the masses of workers, peasants and soldiers. They wildly attack the creative study and application of Mao Tse-tung's works by workers, peasants and sol-diers as "philistinism," "oversimplification" and "prag-matism." The only explanation is that this flows from their exploiting class instinct. They fear Mao Tse-tung's thought, the revolutionary truth of the proletariat, and particularly the integration of Mao Tse-tung's thought with the worker, peasant and soldier masses. Once the workers, peasants and soldiers master the sharp weapon of Mao Tse-tung's thought, all monsters have no ground left to stand on. All their intrigues and plots will be thoroughly exposed, their ugly features will be brought into the broad light of day and their dream to restore capitalism will be utterly shattered.

> The class enemy won't fall down, if you don't hit him.

The class enemy won't fall down, if you don't hit him. He still tries to rise to his feet after he has fallen. When one black line is eliminated, another appears. When one gang of representatives of the bourgeoisie has been laid low, a new one takes the stage. We must follow the in-structions of the Central Committee of the Communist Party of China and never forget the class struggle, never forget the dictatorship of the proletariat, never forget to put politics first, never forget to hold aloft the great red banner of Mao Tse-tung's thought. We must firmly put politics first. We must creatively study and apply still better Chairman Mao Tse-tung's works, putting stress on the importance of application. We must consider Chairman Mao's works the supreme directive for all our work. We must master Mao Tse-tung's thought and pass it on from generation to generation. This is dictated by the needs of the revolution, the situation, the struggle against the enemy, the preparations to smash aggressive war by U.S. imperialism, of opposing and preventing revisionism, preventing the restoration of capitalism, of building socialism with greater, faster, better and more economical results and of ensuring the gradual transition from socialism to communism in China. Chairman Mao is the radiant sun lighting our minds. Mao Tse-tung's thought is our lifeline. Those who oppose Mao Tse-tung's thought, at any time and no matter what kind of "authorities" they are, will be denounced by the entire Party and the whole nation.

Chinese High School Students Begin a New Era

Beijing No. 26 Middle School Red Guards

Groups of activist young people known as Red Guards played the largest and most visible part in the Chinese Cultural Revolution. As Mao Zedong and other leaders began to speak and write of a continuing revolution in 1966, groups of Red Guards formed on their own, without official sanction, and the movement quickly spread. Mao succeeded in harnessing their energy to his own cause, while the Red Guards themselves proclaimed their loyalty and devotion to him loudly and often. From 1966 to 1969, bands of Red Guards transformed schools, destroyed ancient monuments, rejected the ways of their parents, and attacked those not thought to be "revolutionary" enough. The following selection is a list of ways in which

SOURCE. Beijing No. 26 Middle School Red Guards, "One Hundred Items for Destroying the Old and Establishing the New," *China's Cultural Revolution, 1966–1969: Not a Dinner Party, Chinese Sociology and Anthropology: A Journal of Translations.* Armonk, NY: M.E. Sharpe, v. 2, no. 3–4, Spring–Summer 1970, 1996, pp. 212–222. Copyright © 1996 by M.E. Sharpe. All rights reserved. Reproduced by permission.

the Red Guards of Beijing's No. 26 Middle School (Chinese middle school is roughly equivalent to high school in the United States) wanted to help Mao destroy the old society and inaugurate a new one. Fairly randomly organized, the group's one hundred demands touch on topics ranging from family life to popular culture to commerce. A common emphasis is on the need to place "Mao Zedong Thought" at the center of any transformation.

1. Under the charge of residential committees, every street must set up a quotation plaque; every household must have on its walls a picture of the Chairman plus quotations by Chairman Mao.

2. More quotations by Chairman Mao must be put up in the parks. Ticket takers on buses and conductors on trains should make the propagation of Mao Zedong Thought and the reading of Chairman Mao's quotations their primary task.

3. The management bureaus of publishing enterprises must mainly print Chairman Mao's works, and most of the sales of New China bookstores must make the radiance of Mao Zedong Thought shine in every corner of the whole country.

4. Printing companies must print quotations by the Chairman in large numbers; they must be sold in every bookstore until there is a copy of the *Quotations from Chairman Mao* in the hands of everyone in the whole country.

5. With a copy of the *Quotations from Chairman Mao* in the hands of everyone, each must carry it with him, constantly study it, and do everything in accord with it.

6. Fine art publishing companies must print large batches of stock quotations by the Chairman. Especially on anniversary occasions, they must sell great quantities of quotations and revolutionary couplets—enough to satisfy the needs of the people.

7. Plaques of quotations by the Chairman must be hung on all available bicycles and pedicabs; pictures

> Pictures of the Chairman must be hung and Chairman Mao's sayings painted on motor vehicles and trains.

of the Chairman must be hung and Chairman Mao's sayings painted on motor vehicles and trains.

8. The relevant departments must manufacture bicycle and pedicab quotation plaques on a scale large enough to meet the needs of the people.

9. Newly manufactured products such as bicycles, motor vehicles, trains, airplanes, etc., must uniformly bear quotation plaques. This procedure must be increased, not decreased.

10. Neighborhood work must put Mao Zedong Thought in first place, must set up small groups for the study of Chairman Mao's works, and must revolutionize housewives.

11. Every school and every unit must set up highest directive propaganda teams so that everyone can hear at any time the repeated instructions of the Chairman.

12. Broadcasting units must be set up in every park and at every major intersection, and, under the organizational responsibility of such organs as the Red Guards, propagate Mao Zedong Thought and current international and national events.

13. The old national anthem absolutely must be reformed by the workers, peasants, and soldiers into a eulogy to the Party and Chairman Mao. . . .

14. Neighborhood residential committees must put up several newspaper display cases so that everyone can take an interest in major national and world events.

15. From now on every newspaper must put Mao Zedong Thought in first place. Editorials must be few and to the point, and there must be more good articles dealing with the living study and living application of the Chairman's works by the workers, peasants, and soldiers.

16. Letters and stamps must never have bourgeois things printed on them (such as cats, dogs, or other ar-

tistic things). Politics must be predominant. A quotation by Chairman Mao or a militant utterance by a hero must be printed on every envelope.

17. When members of companies celebrate brigade days, they are not permitted to visit parks. They must strengthen their class education and their education in Mao Zedong Thought.

18. Hereafter on the national day, everyone must carry a copy of the Chairman's quotations and a bouquet, and the bouquets must be arranged in slogans.

19. Shop windows cannot be dominated by displays of scents and perfumes. They must be decorated with simplicity and dignity and must put Mao Zedong Thought first.

20. Theaters must have a strong political atmosphere. Before the movie starts, quotations from Chairman Mao must be shown. Don't let the bourgeoisie rule our stages. Cut the superfluous hooligan scenes, and reduce the price of tickets on behalf of the workers, peasants, and soldiers.

21. Literary and art workers must energetically model in clay heroic images of workers, peasants, and soldiers engaged in living study and living application of Chairman Mao's works. Their works must be pervaded by the one red line of Mao Zedong Thought.

22. All professional literary and art teams must gradually be transformed into Mao Zedong Thought propaganda teams like the *Ulanmuqi* [cultural team] and the "Sea-Borne Cultural Workers' Company"; they must be highly proletarianized, highly militant, and highly ideologized.

23. Our nation has already been established for seventeen years. But those who drank the blood of the people and oppressed the people before the Liberation, those bourgeois bastards, are still collecting fixed interest and interest from stocks and living the lives of parasites. We warn you: Immediately desist from collecting fixed

interest and interest from stocks; you are only allowed to honestly reform your bastardly ideology—you are not permitted to exploit the people.

24. You landowners who still rode on the people's heads and drank the people's blood after the Liberation, we order you bastards to hurry up and turn over all your private holdings to the state. In a socialist state we absolutely cannot allow you vampires to exist.

25. In a proletarian society, private enterprise cannot be allowed to exist. We propose to take all firms using joint state and private management and change them to state management and change joint state and private management enterprises into state-owned enterprises.

26. Our socialist society absolutely cannot allow any hoodlums or juvenile delinquents to exist. We order you right this minute to get rid of your blue jeans, shave off your slick hairdos, take off your rocket shoes, and quit your black organizations. Peking [Beijing] is the heart of world revolution. It is not the big world you squatted on before the Liberation. We warn you: You are not allowed to go on recklessly doing your evil deeds—if you do, you will be responsible for the consequences.

> Clothing stores are firmly prohibited from making tight pants, Hong Kong-style suits, weird women's outfits, and grotesque men's suits.

27. All who are in service trades are not permitted to serve the bourgeoisie. Clothing stores are firmly prohibited from making tight pants, Hong Kong-style suits, weird women's outfits, and grotesque men's suits. All revolutionary comrades in service trades must strictly adhere to this.

28. All daily necessities (perfume, snowflake cream [facial moisturizer], etc.) that do not serve the broad worker, peasant, and soldier masses must be prohibited from sale right away. Merchandise trademark designs must be radically changed.

29. Photography studios must serve the broad worker, peasant, soldier masses and must abolish the taking of profile photos and all kinds of grotesque pictures. Display windows should be arranged with large, simple photos of workers, peasants, and soldiers.

30. Stop producing poker cards, military chess, and all other such things that advertise bourgeois ideology.

31. Trading stores cannot sell secondhand clothes, Western clothes, or any other ridiculous things the bourgeoisie love to see.

32. Laundries must cease washing pants, stockings, and handkerchiefs for those bourgeois wives, misses, and young gentlemen and completely crush their stuck-up airs. Do not yield to their senseless demands; you should greatly enhance the pride of the proletariat and utterly destroy bourgeois pomp.

33. Public baths must consistently desist from serving those bourgeois sons of bitches. Don't give them massage baths, footrubs, backrubs; don't let them bow our heads again, or abuse and ride roughshod over us.

34. Bookstores for classical books must this minute stop doing business. Children's bookstores must immediately destroy all pornographic children's books, and all bookstores and libraries must be internally purified and must clear away all poisonous weeds; do not permit these goods of the bourgeois ideology to be poured into our youth ever again.

35. All the landlords, rich-peasants, counter-revolutionaries, hooligans, Rightists, and other members of the bourgeois class are not permitted to collect pornographic books and decadent records. Whoever violates this rule will, when discovered, be treated as guilty of attempting to restore the old order, and his collections will be destroyed.

36. Children must sing revolutionary songs. Those rotten tunes of the cat and dog variety must never again waft in the air of our socialist state. In this great socialist

state of ours, absolutely no one is allowed to play games of chance.

37. The bastards of the bourgeoisie are not allowed to hire governesses. Whoever dares to violate or resist this rule and thus continues to ride on the heads of the laboring people will be severely punished.

38. All service industries must turn their faces toward the workers, peasants, and soldiers. They must bear a class nature; they cannot produce anything for the service of the bourgeoisie.

39. Every hospital must turn its face toward the workers, peasants, and soldiers. They must reform the old system and abolish the registration system.

40. Peddlers who make little toys to deceive and, in a disguised form, poison children, we order you to stop business right away. Not the least consideration will be shown toward those who violate this order. In addition,

Students, considered by Mao to be the leaders of the revolution, march to their next lesson at a secondary school in 1973. (Keystone/Getty Images.)

we order toy shops immediately to stop selling small toys such as watches, etc., that advertise bourgeois ideology.

41. Every industrial enterprise must abolish the bourgeois bonus award system. In this great socialist nation of ours, the broad worker, peasant, soldier masses, armed with the great Mao Zedong Thought, have no need for material incentives.

42. Heads of families are not allowed to educate their children with bourgeois ideology. The feudal family-head system will be abolished. No more beating or scolding of children will be tolerated. If the child is not of one's own begetting, no mistreatment is allowed. Children will be consistently educated in Mao Zedong Thought.

43. Cricket raising and cricket fights will no longer be permitted. The raising of fish, cats, and dogs and other such bourgeois habits shall not exist in the midst of the Chinese people. Whoever breaks this rule will be responsible for the consequences.

> You old bastards of the bourgeoisie . . . are ordered to lower your high salaries to the level of those of the workers.

44. You old bastards of the bourgeoisie who receive high salaries, listen well: Before Liberation you rode on the heads of the people, sometimes severe, sometimes lenient. Now you still receive salaries many times more than ten times higher than those of the workers. You are thus drinking the blood of the people—you are guilty. Starting in September [1966], you are ordered to lower your high salaries to the level of those of the workers. Landlords, rich-peasants, counter-revolutionaries, hooligans, and Rightists who have deposits in banks are not allowed to take even a penny for themselves. Whoever breaks this rule is responsible for the consequences—there will not be the least politeness.

45. Scoundrels of the bourgeoisie are not allowed to wander around or visit parks at will. The monthly tickets of those who have bought them to visit parks or ride

Mao's *Little Red Book*

The central text of the Cultural Revolution was a compilation known as Quotations from Chairman Mao Tse-Tung, *which first appeared in 1964. During the years of the Revolution, it was published in a small size with a red cover and came to be known familiarly simply as the* Little Red Book. *Devotees such as the Red Guards commonly carried copies with them at all times, taking pride in memorizing selections. In the agricultural communes where urbanites were often "sent down" to rural areas to experience the lives of peasants, the workday often ended with the singing of folk songs based on such statements from the* Little Red Book *as these:*

A revolution is not a dinner party, or writing an essay, or painting a picture, or doing embroidery; it cannot be so refined, so leisurely and gentle, so temperate, kind, courteous, restrained, and magnanimous. A revolution is an insurrection, an act of violence by which one class overthrows another.

What is work? Work is struggle. There are difficulties and problems in those places for us to overcome and solve. We go there to work and struggle to overcome these difficulties. A good comrade is one who is more eager to go where difficulties are greater.

The enemy will not perish of himself. Neither will the Chinese reactionaries nor the aggressive forces of U.S. imperialism in China step down from the stage of history of their own accord.

All reactionaries are paper tigers. In appearance, the reactionaries are terrifying, but in reality they are not so powerful. From a long-term point of view, it is not the reactionaries but the people who are powerful.

in cars as a way to enjoy their leisure will be destroyed. They cannot indulge in wild fancies.

46. Except for the old, the weak, the sick, and the crippled who may ride in pedicabs, the bastards of the bourgeoisie are forbidden to ride in pedicabs. Whoever

violates this rule will be handled with severity. The number of pedicab workers must be reduced, and suitable arrangements for good jobs will be made.

47. Landlords, rich-peasants, counter-revolutionaries, hooligans, Rightists, and capitalists, when they go out, must wear plaques as monsters and freaks under the supervision of the masses. Whoever violates this rule will be dealt with severely.

> **Whoever violates this rule will be dealth with severly.**

48. All monsters and freaks and puppets of the "Black Gang" [groups opposed to the Cultural Revolution] are forbidden to receive salaries without the approval of the masses. We want to lower the salaries of these old bastards. The scoundrels will get only enough to keep them alive.

49. Restaurants can no longer be places where the bastards of the bourgeoisie go to eat, drink, and enjoy themselves. Service personnel are not allowed to respond to their senseless demands and prepare for them delicacies from the mountains and seas. The finger guessing game cannot be played in restaurants. No service may be rendered these bastards.

50. Factories must not give pensions to landlords, rich-peasants, counter-revolutionaries, hooligans, and Rightists. Their payments and benefits will all be abolished, and they will be required to labor under the supervision of the masses.

51. The bastards of the bourgeoisie are not permitted to occupy a large number of houses, the [minimum] limit being three persons to one room. The surplus rooms shall be turned over to the Housing Bureau for management, lest we take action.

52. All those of the five categories of landlords, rich-peasants, counter-revolutionaries, hooligans, and Rightists who are jobless shall go back to their native place to engage in production.

53. Social youth who loaf around, we order you: Register immediately at the employment office and go to the frontier territories to participate in labor and production.

54. From now on, police stations are not allowed to find jobs in the cities for those who don't adhere to the state assignments. Let them go to the frontier territories.

55. Old bastards of the bourgeoisie, we order you instantly to hand over to the government all the money you took by exploitation before Liberation. You vampires are no longer allowed to squander at will.

56. Wrestling areas throughout the country will be disbanded, and the wrestlers will go to police stations to register for participation in labor. You can no longer poison the people.

57. We order magicians throughout the country who depend on deceiving the people for a living: Stop your business immediately; go to police stations to register!

> The family-head system shall be destroyed, and children may make suggestions to grownups.

58. All circus and theater programs must be changed. They must put on meaningful things. Actors are not allowed to dress up in strange fashions, because we don't need those filthy things.

59. We order all those young rabbits who have not joined pedicab associations and are driving black pedicabs (i.e., those who go out during the night to train or bus stations, large streets, and small alleys to look for customers and who unnecessarily pass through large streets and small alleys to stretch the mere two *li* of the original distance to five in order to charge twice as much) to immediately stop engaging in this kind of criminal business and to submit themselves to the bureaus of public safety.

60. All those athletic activities that don't correspond with practical significance will be appropriately reduced. Physical education for national defense, such as swimming, mountain climbing, shooting, etc., will be greatly

developed so that gradually every youth or adult over fifteen years of age will have a range of enemy-killing abilities. All the people are soldiers, always prepared to annihilate the invading enemy.

61. Those who repair shoes on large streets and small alleys, we order you to stop doing business at once. Under the responsible organs, organize yourselves into shoe-repair associations. The price for shoe repairs must be reduced.

62. Nobody may address letters to "Sir" so and so. The whole range of feudal practices must be abolished and new customs advocated.

63. The limousines, television sets, and motorcycles in households of "five category-elements" and "Black Gang" elements shall all be confiscated. Television sets will be turned over to residential committees, who will then give them to the families of the workers, peasants, and soldiers to watch.

64. From now on, no newspapers are allowed to give excessive payments for writing articles. This hole of black wind shall be stopped up.

65. The family-head system shall be destroyed, and children may make suggestions to grownups.

66. Hospitals must not charge in advance for emergency treatment (excepting "five category-elements"). Complicated treatment must be abolished. Specific reforms will be left for the medical workers to decide. The old and Western frameworks shall be smashed, and everything will serve the people.

67. All the monsters and freaks (old bureaucrats, landlords, capitalists, hooligans, etc.) are prohibited from teaching the traditional military skills, boxing, and internal hygiene in parks or other places.

68. All broadcasts of literary and art performances and movies shall immediately eliminate the names of authors, actors, conductors, etc. This road to individual fame and profit will thus be blocked.

> We order those under thirty-five to quit smoking and drinking immediately.

69. We order those under thirty-five to quit drinking and smoking immediately. Bad habits of this sort absolutely may not be cultivated.

70. Telling dirty jokes, uttering profanities, and doing vulgar things are strictly forbidden. Violators will be severely dealt with. The bad habits of using nicknames, job titles, etc., are strictly forbidden. Everyone shall be called comrade (with the exception of the "five black categories").

71. Advanced elements of the workers, peasants, and soldiers are responsible for being street activists. Bourgeois elements will not be allowed to usurp their roles.

72. From now on, postmen will not deliver letters upstairs or into compounds. Letter boxes will be prepared inside multistored buildings. For large compounds, a special man will be found to take on the responsibility. The labor of postmen comrades will be reduced.

73. Resplendent wedding ceremonies are forbidden. There must be no extravagance or squandering. New customs and new habits can be advocated.

74. The wearing of feudal things such as bracelets, earrings, and longevity chains is forbidden.

75. We recommend for the consideration of the responsible organs that the interest system in banking be abolished and the people be allowed to save self-consciously on the basis of patriotism and assistance to socialist construction.

76. We suggest that from now on no admission will be charged to any critical movies and that they be seen by organized groups. There will be no tickets sold to individuals. All elements of the "five black categories" will not be allowed to see these movies.

77. Things left over from the old society, such as buying snacks or fruits while visiting friends or relatives,

will all be abolished. We hope that the worker, peasant, soldier masses will support this movement.

78. Except for urgent and crucial matters, taxis will not be hired. The bastards of the bourgeoisie will not be allowed to ride in these taxis.

79. The responsible organs must do their best to find ways to establish public toilets in the various alleys so as to reduce the heavy work of the sanitation workers.

80. The state must vigorously develop the motor-transportation industry in order to reduce the heavy labor of the cart-pulling workers.

81. From now on, the Changtian Amusement Park will not open during Chinese New Year. We must take account of economics, and we must take account of politics.

82. From now on, all universities, high schools, and vocational schools will be run as communist schools with part-time work and part-time study and part-time farming and part-time study.

83. We students must respond to Chairman Mao's appeal. Students must also learn from the workers, the peasants, and the soldiers, and each year during their vacations they must go to factories, farms, and military camps to train themselves.

84. We are determined to demand reform in the vacation system. Vacations shall be taken during the busy season for the peasants so that we can go to the villages to help in agricultural production.

85. Sofas, couches, etc., may not be produced in great quantities.

86. Expensive articles such as gold pens, etc., shall not be produced in great quantities (except for export) because they do not serve the broad worker, peasant, soldier masses.

87. No manufactured goods in shops may be called by their Western names. Meaningful Chinese names must be used.

88. We appeal to all League members to take off and throw away their League emblems. Get rid of this poisonous weed.

89. When prescribing medicine, doctors must destroy the Western framework of writing in English and clearly explain the type of medicine prescribed. Their signatures have to be legible.

90. We are determined that the youth vanguard corps cannot be allowed to turn into an all-people's corps. Otherwise, it would lose its significance as a vanguard.

91. Schools must use Mao's works as textbooks and educate the youth in Mao Zedong Thought.

92. All schools must have physical training and participation in labor in a primary position and strengthen military training.

93. Schools must destroy the feudal teacher-student etiquette and establish an equal relationship between teacher and student.

> Schools must destroy the feudal teacher-student etiquette and establish an equal relationship between teacher and student.

94. Starting this year, normal colleges, normal schools [that train teachers], and schools for training primary school teachers must absorb the sons and daughters of the "five red elements" into their schools.

95. Those who have names with feudal bourgeois overtones will voluntarily go to police stations to change their names.

96. No fences or small houses are allowed to be built inside or outside a garden. The growth of such selfish thoughts must not be encouraged.

97. Abolish the system of the sale of annual tickets for parks. If the workers, peasants, and soldiers need to rest, all tickets will be distributed to them by factories and agencies.

98. We suggest that the state consider a universal increase in wages of the workers and a decrease in wages for the authorities of the bourgeoisie.

99. "Black Gang" elements shall be fined according to their criminal acts.

100. Advocate simplified characters. From now on, all newspapers and other publications will use simplified characters in their headlines.

The Maoism School (originally No. 26 Middle School) Red Guards

[August 1966]

China Declassifies Documents from the Cultural Revolution Era

Xiyun Yang and Michael Wines

China's government, despite capitalist reforms that have helped the nation quickly grow into the world's second largest economy, remains Communist. Leaders maintain careful control over the flow of information, including information on the Cultural Revolution. As journalists Xiyun Yang and Michael Wines note in the following article, however, China's government is beginning to make available official documents and other records of that era, though the files have been filtered for any mention of death and imprisonment. The article, first published in 2010, describes how these newly available records are allowing historians to build a more varied, colorful story of those days. The documents will also allow China's young people, who have almost no knowledge of the Cultural Revolution, to learn more fully what their parents and grandparents went through in the 1960s and 1970s, the authors say.

I t was the height of the Cultural Revolution, but in the heart of China's capital, in range of the prying eyes of foreign embassies, young Beijingers had embraced the tenets of capitalism.

Corrupted by dreams of profit, crowds of 500 or more were gathering every Sunday on a street in Beijing's embassy district to ply a shameful trade. "They are learning how to do business and raise money," one city official wrote darkly. "This is seriously harmful to the healthy growth of the successors of the proletariat revolution."

Such was the state of affairs in 1966, when selling pigeons at an impromptu street market was seen as an obstacle to the triumph of socialism—and, the official added, as a waste of bird feed, too.

The records on the Beijing pigeon market, like thousands of other Cultural Revolution documents, lay silent for decades, deemed state secrets by a government hardly eager to highlight Mao Zedong's excesses. But last year, China quietly opened the archives of selected declassified government files from that era, in Beijing, Shanghai and Xian.

> Today, that era has been all but obliterated from the official history of the People's Republic, its horrors glossed over in history books.

And so a veil has begun to lift on this and other prosaic stories of the Cultural Revolution—some sad, some funny, most humdrum to an extreme.

The files of the Cultural Revolution, which raged from 1966 until Mao's death in 1976, make up a mere 16 of the 21,568 volumes that the Beijing Municipal Archives has made public in four separate releases—in

1996, 1997, 2001 and 2009. (The other files cover periods of Chinese history from 1906.) Stored in thick binders on library-style stacks, they can be viewed in the Municipal Archives building, a spacious, modern structure with overstuffed chairs and a scholarly atmosphere on the south side of the city.

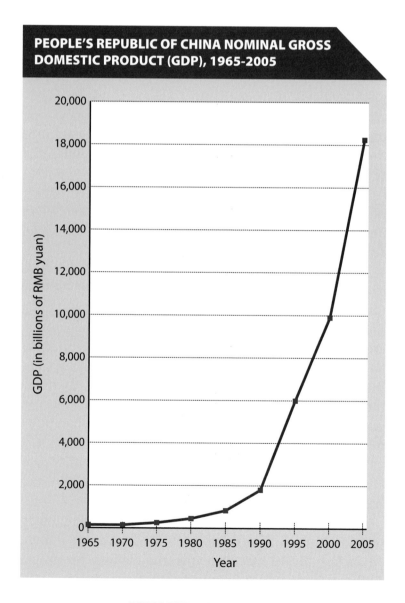

PEOPLE'S REPUBLIC OF CHINA NOMINAL GROSS DOMESTIC PRODUCT (GDP), 1965-2005

The yellowing files give scant insight into those days' atrocities: the denunciations of parents by children; the humiliation of intellectuals; the millions of lives ruined by Red Guards ordered to remake society through upheaval. Mao's personality cult made him a living god, and armed violence broke out over his affections. Everything was politicized. Many committed suicide.

Today, that era has been all but obliterated from the official history of the People's Republic, its horrors glossed over in history books. While many younger Chinese know that the country passed through a period of turmoil, scholars say, few have any idea of its wild extremes.

Events that were "earth shattering have now turned into words with vague and sketchy meanings," Chen Xiaojing, a Communist Party official from the time, wrote in a carefully hedged account of his experiences, "My Cultural Revolution Years."

> 'Mao Zedong Thought' cured everything from truancy to traffic jams to agricultural chemistry to illegal pigeon sales.

Why the government is releasing some documents from the era is unclear. Archive officials declined repeated requests for interviews. Experts say the files contain little if any material that government censors would regard as incendiary.

"For people like me who have been studying the Cultural Revolution as a profession, it's better than having nothing at all," said Xu Youyu, a historian and former researcher at the Chinese Academy of Social Sciences. "But the things I want to know are—for example, how many homes the Red Guards had gone to raid and what they took out of each home—there's not a chance of finding those things in these documents.

"If you air these things out, people may start asking why it happened. And this is not a question that is directed only at 1966, but may be turned around and asked about the current situation in China."

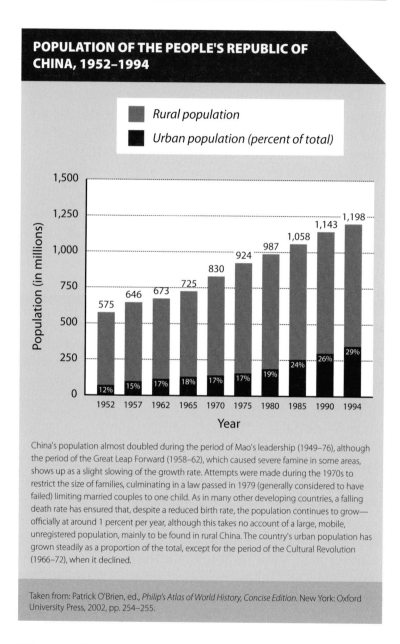

POPULATION OF THE PEOPLE'S REPUBLIC OF CHINA, 1952–1994

Legend:
- Rural population
- Urban population (percent of total)

China's population almost doubled during the period of Mao's leadership (1949–76), although the period of the Great Leap Forward (1958–62), which caused severe famine in some areas, shows up as a slight slowing of the growth rate. Attempts were made during the 1970s to restrict the size of families, culminating in a law passed in 1979 (generally considered to have failed) limiting married couples to one child. As in many other developing countries, a falling death rate has ensured that, despite a reduced birth rate, the population continues to grow—officially at around 1 percent per year, although this takes no account of a large, mobile, unregistered population, mainly to be found in rural China. The country's urban population has grown steadily as a proportion of the total, except for the period of the Cultural Revolution (1966–72), when it declined.

Taken from: Patrick O'Brien, ed., *Philip's Atlas of World History, Concise Edition*. New York: Oxford University Press, 2002, pp. 254–255.

Hints of a Strange Time

Yet a picture of Chinese life 40 and 50 years ago does emerge from the archives. The files, some nearly transparent and thin as one-ply tissue paper, include handwritten drafts of speeches, lists of production quotas, song lyrics, government regulations and minutes of groups that studied Mao's words. The texts embrace the political rhetoric of the day, in which all problems were succinctly rendered into rhyming epithets.

The files apparently have been filtered for anything dealing with deaths and imprisonment, and they describe a country still fervently Communist, and unrecognizable today. They narrate the story of a country in the throes of madness, when "Mao Zedong Thought" cured everything from truancy to traffic jams to agricultural chemistry to illegal pigeon sales.

Consider: records from 1972, taken at a grade school outside Beijing, show that math students were made to sing two revolutionary songs and study and discuss six Mao quotations for 25 minutes of each class. The remaining few minutes were spent doing math.

In 1967, a report urged forming special groups at the provincial and city levels to "use every conceivable means to guarantee production" each year of 13,000 tons of specially formulated red plastic—required for the covers of Mao's "Little Red Book" of quotations.

"The Conference on the Situation of the Special Plastic Used by the Works of Chairman Mao" proclaimed that producing the plastic was "our glorious political responsibility." To hold everyone accountable, the conference produced a chart with a month-by-month breakdown of production levels.

At times, the files veer perilously close to black, or perhaps red, comedy. In 1970, the annual Representative Conference of the Enthusiasts of Chairman Mao's Works from the City Transportation Bureau studied rush-hour bottlenecks created because workers were required to arrive early to study Chairman Mao's works. The bottlenecks, the workers concluded, were the work of "conservative rightists and selfish departmentalism and other mistaken ideas."

A Buddhist monk walks among the ruins of the Gedan Songzan Monastery at Zhongdian. It was destroyed by the Red Guards during a two-week spree in 1966. (AP Photo/Greg Baker.)

Yet there are also oblique hints of more sinister processes at work.

Many reports began with anecdotes of selfless revolutionary fervor. In one of them, Liu Chunnong, a transportation security guard, recounted in 1968 how his dozen pet goldfish had been his pride and joy. After a party meeting, he said, he took the fish outside and buried them alive. Raising goldfish, he wrote, had been criticized as a petit bourgeois practice.

In a handwritten series of 1972 speeches, many of them heavily edited in pen, a teacher from Beijing's outskirts recalled how his comrades "patiently and delicately" sought to reform a teacher who was not a worker, but a member of the wealthy class. Rounds of criticism had little effect, so the group chose to help him realize his mistakes through physical labor, by weeding farmland.

"He pulled grass," the speech read. "At first, he was squatting, but he couldn't handle it after two days. Then he pulled the grass while kneeling. Finally, he did it while crawling."

Party censors excised the tale of the exhausted teacher from the final draft of the speech.

CHAPTER 2

Controversies Surrounding the Chinese Cultural Revolution

Reverence for Mao Zedong Lay at the Heart of the Cultural Revolution

Liu Xiaoqing

The following selection was written by one of China's most famous film actresses of the 1980s and 1990s. Liu Xiaoqing was born in 1952, which made her just the right age to become an active and enthusiastic participant in the Cultural Revolution. In this selection, taken from her 1992 memoir, Liu emphasizes the importance of Mao Zedong as both the symbol of and leader of China's attempted transformation during the Cultural Revolution. She describes how Mao received the sort of adulation from her fellow teenagers that teenagers in the West gave to actors and musicians, and how Mao's words and teachings were the foundation of the Cultural Revolution. Although too young to be a Red Guard, she remembers joining a related group known as the Red Brigades and how, during a visit to

Photo on previous page: A poster in Beijing shows how the Red Guards would deal with so-called enemies of the people. (Jean Vincent/AFP/Getty Images.)

Beijing's Tiananmen Square, she once glimpsed Mao personally. A later visit to Mao's mausoleum brought back memories of her childhood and how much a part of it China's leader had been. Liu Xiaoqing's films include *A Dream in Red Mansions* and *The Dowager Empress*. She is also one of China's wealthiest businesswomen.

I've only seen Mao Zedong twice. On the first occasion he was standing, the second time he was flat on his back. The first time he was on Tiananmen Gate to review the Red Guards who, like me, had travelled to Beijing to see him. The second time was at the Chairman Mao Memorial Hall where I lined up to view his body.

Everyone says that you never forget your first love. I can't really say that I ever had a first love, for in my childhood and youth the man I loved and admired most of all was Mao Zedong. I gave him everything I had: my sincerest love, as well as all my longing and hopes. He was an idol I worshipped with all my heart.

Chairman Mao, you were my first object of desire!

The first song I learnt to sing was "The East is Red". I knew what Chairman Mao looked like from the time I could recognize my parents. When I was a Red Guard I could recite all of his quotations word perfect. My brain was armed with Mao Zedong Thought. During the unprecedented Cultural Revolution I used Chairman Mao's words as my weapon to parry with opponents. My prodigious memory and quick tongue always meant that my "enemies" would retreat in defeat.

If I ever had any problems I would search Chairman Mao's writings for an answer. When we lost one of our chicks I looked for help in his works. When, not long after, the chick reappeared, I knew it was due to the intercession of our Great, Wise and Correct Chairman Mao.

When, as a child, I played games with my friends our pledge of honour was: "I swear by Chairman Mao".

If someone said that, even if they prefaced it by claiming that they'd just come from Mars, we'd believe it without question. Naturally, no one ever took this oath lightly.

I worshipped and loved Chairman Mao so utterly that there was absolutely nothing extraneous or impure in my feelings for him. When I grew a bit older and learnt the secret of how men and women make babies I had the most shocking realization: "Could Chairman Mao possibly do that as well?" Of course, I immediately banished this sacrilegious thought from my head. . . .

> Chairman Mao set the revolutionary blaze of the Cultural Revolution alight. It also ignited our youthful enthusiasm.

Then Chairman Mao set the revolutionary blaze of the Cultural Revolution alight. It also ignited our youthful enthusiasm. We were like moths drawn to a flame and we threw ourselves into the inferno en masse. We were in a frenzy and utilized every ounce of energy at our disposal.

We would give anything to protect Chairman Mao, including our very lives. Our love for the Chairman consumed us body and soul. If anyone had dared to try and harm our beloved Chairman we would have pounced on him, bitten his hand off, gouged out his eyes, screamed in his ears until he was deaf, spat on him until he drowned in a lake of spittle and would have happily died in the effort just like [the revolutionary martyr] Dong Cunrui.

Mao Visits the Red Guards

On 18 August 1968, Chairman Mao reviewed the Red Guards for the first time. I was too young to become a Red Guard, but I spent all my time dreaming of joining the organization that was sworn to protect Chairman Mao. After making extraordinary efforts I was finally allowed to take part in a peripheral grouping called the "Red Brigade". They gave me a red armband too. It was like a dream come true. Although it wasn't the same as the Red Guards, but the difference was only one word. I wore it so the word "Brigade" was hidden under my arm. I stuck out my chest and, just like a real Red Guard, strutted around the school yard incredibly proud of myself.

Soon after that, Chairman Mao called on the Red Guards to travel around China on Revolutionary Linkups. Our group of Red Brigade members decided to respond to Chairman Mao's call too. Without a penny to our names, and each carrying a yellow-green PLA [People's Liberation Army] napsack that we had all done our darnedest to get a hold of (including some who had dyed their own bags), we set out. I had cut off my beloved pigtails so I looked like the revolutionary Sister Jiang [a character from a Chinese opera]. At the train station, we fought our way past all the people who tried to persuade us to "return to the classroom and continue the revolution there". Pushing them aside with determined urgency we got onto the train. With a great clamour the train moved out of the station. We were in very high-spirits, our hearts throbbing with revolutionary ardour. Then one of my classmates asked: "Where are we going?" I was stunned and asked the others: "Where's this train headed?" We took out a map of China and put our heads together and, doing our best to put the basics of geography we'd just acquired in class to use, we scrutinized the map and finally worked out that we were on the Baocheng line. There would be a change of locomotive at Baoji and the train would then head for Beijing.

Beijing! The city where Chairman Mao lived! We went wild.

Over the next few days, we were so excited about going to Beijing that we didn't sleep a wink. But where would Chairman Mao be? Would we be able to see him? We all stood atop the "Gold Mountain of Beijing" which we had dreamed of for so long, tormented by these questions.

We imitated the Red Guards of Beijing scrupulously, literally aping their every move. When we got on a bus we would take out *Quotations from Chairman Mao* and start reading in really loud voices. "Revolution is not a tea party. It is not like writing an essay, painting or embroidering flowers, . . . revolution is an act of violence, it is the violent overthrow of one class by another. . . ." We did our best to make our heavily-accented Sichuan voices sound as much like Beijing dialect as we could. We'd read one quotation after another right to the end of the trip. . . .

I will never forget August 31, 1966. On that day I joined all the Red Guards who had come from throughout China to be in Beijing to see him, to see Chairman

Actress Liu Xiaoqing comes out for a curtain call during her stage drama *The Last Night of Taipan Chin* in Guangzhou. (China Photos/Getty Images.)

Mao, the leader we dreamt of and thought of 24 hours a day.

A few days earlier we had been told by the Revolutionary Committee of the Agricultural Museum that some Central leaders would see us on August 31. When we heard this everyone exploded in excitement. Speculation was rife: which leader or leaders would be there? Would Chairman Mao come? The result of our group deliberations was that Chairman Mao was sure to be too busy to come. Since we were from out of Beijing there was even less reason for him to see us. But there was a small and adamant group who were sure that Chairman Mao would appear. Naturally, I really wanted to believe them. Truth, after all, [as Chairman Mao taught us] is often the prerogative of the minority.

It was 6:00 A.M., August 31. We all woke with a start. Although we were all at the age when you find it impossible to wake up in the morning, everyone had been really excited the night before. People had woken at the slightest noise and looked around to see that nothing was going on before drifting off to sleep again. But this time it was for real. We all got dressed in record time and, armed with the food and water we had set aside the night before, we ran into the courtyard.

Children Wait to See Chairman Mao

Once assembled, we got into our bus and were driven to Tiananmen Square. We lined up and sat in ranks; the Square was turned into a massive sea of green. We waited wide-eyed and expectant. Morning broke slowly and we saw the majestic outline of Tiananmen Gate. As the sun rose we began to get hot. But we waited, and waited. Our eyes were popping out of our heads. The sweat trickled down our brows and into our eyes. Everyone was constantly wiping the sweat away with their hands. We took out our food and water and started chatting as we ate. Some people nodded off to sleep, heads cushioned on their knees. As a person nodded, their head might slip off their knee and they'd wake with a shock, look around and then nod off again. This happened repeatedly. Some people simply lay down to sleep using their caps and satchels as a pillow. I stood up and looked out over the Square, a massive expanse occupied by an army of battle-weary Red Guards. I sat down and was overcome by drowsiness myself and, despite my best efforts to keep awake, I nodded off.

> The eyes of a million Red Guards were riveted on Tiananmen Gate.

Suddenly, drums could be heard, a weak sound at first that grew louder. After the drum roll, all the loudspeakers on the Square resounded with the opening chords of "The East is Red," followed by the tumultous din of the orchestral arrangement of the song. The very earth shook with the volume of sound. Everyone jumped to their feet. My heart was in my throat, I could feel my pulse around my lips, in my head and neck. The eyes of a million Red Guards were riveted on Tiananmen Gate.

The leaders of Party Central had appeared! But who was behind them? It was Chairman Mao himself!! Everyone threw down their hats, satchels, bread, water flasks and began shouting as we surged towards Tiananmen. All those acres of green-clad bodies that had been sitting passively only a moment before turned into a solid wave of human flesh, like a wall of football players. We all shouted "Long Live Chairman Mao!" At first it was an uncoordinated cry but slowly we began chanting in unison. The love that tens of thousands of Red Guards felt for their leader burst forth like a lava flow from Mount Vesuvius. It was like a torrent, like an explosion of liquid steel. Without a second thought I joined in and tears streamed from my eyes. I hated the people in front of me who blocked my line of vision and kept Chairman Mao from me. I hated the fact that I was shortsighted, that at this most precious moment I couldn't see the Chairman clearly. I begged a Red Guard in front of me to lend me his telescope. He was staring into it looking intently at the rostrum on the Gate. Tears had flowed down his cheeks to the corners of his mouth and were dripping onto his clothes. His face was ecstatic. I pleaded with him to let me have one, quick look. "Just for a minute or even only a second. I'll give it back immediately, I swear. I swear by Chairman Mao." He finally gave in and handed me the telescope. I put it up to my eye as quickly as possible but I couldn't find the Chairman anywhere. What was wrong? He wasn't there.

Then suddenly the human wave surged in my direction and I was thrown to the ground. I was held down by a mass of hysterical Red Guards. I pressed down with both arms to keep myself from being crushed, still the breath was knocked out of me. I struggled for all I was worth, but I could feel my strength being sapped away. I couldn't keep up and my face was being forced against the ground, my cheek crushed downwards. I could hear my bones creaking, but I couldn't scream out. I was afraid I would die without ever having seen Chairman Mao. What a wasted life! But my instinct for self-preservation took over and I started fighting my way out, regardless of the cost.

> I was afraid I would die without ever having seen Chairman Mao. What a wasted life!

Miraculously, the crowd in front of me parted and a wide road appeared. In that instant I saw Chairman Mao. He was in an open limousine that was moving slowly in our direction. He was like a statue, as tall as the heavens. He was dressed in military uniform and he waved at us. Tens of thousands of eyes turned towards us, saw our faces, our bodies and saw into our hearts. I went limp but I was held up by the mass of other Red Guards. I felt warm all over; I was drunk with happiness. My tears soaked the front of my army-green uniform. I forgot everything, my studies, my future. Life seemed so unimportant, irrelevant. Nothing could compare with this instant, because I had seen him!

I did, nonetheless, have one major regret. I didn't get a chance to shake Chairman Mao's hand. How I wished I could have become a spirit or a martial arts expert and jumped over the crowd to sit next to Chairman Mao! But I couldn't. The people who shook Chairman Mao's hand that day were our heroes. We all rushed up to them so we could hold them by the hand, reluctant to let go, we nearly tore them to pieces.

A More Mature View

Even today, whenever I hear "The East is Red", that incredibly familiar tune, my heart beats faster. It's because that moment was so profound, so exciting and happy. I've only felt like that once in my whole life. I'm sure I will never, ever feel like that again. . . .

Some years later, I went to Beijing with my mother. One day, we visited the Chairman Mao Mausoleum. Over the years people have ceaselessly gone to see the Chairman's corpse. Our line was like a coiled dragon which wound around the centre of the Square.

Mao Zedong was lying there so still and quiet, at repose in his crystal sarcophagus. The flag of the People's Republic was draped over his body, his face had a peaceful expression on it. I felt an odd mixture of emotions: bitter, sweet, sour and hot. I couldn't take my eyes off him, my leader.

In my mind's eye, I saw him make the announcement: "The People's Republic of China is hereby established. The people of China have stood up!" I saw him dressed in a military uniform waving a cap in his hand as he said: "Long live the People!"

I saw him in his limousine driving towards the hysterical Red Guards.

I saw him standing there with that expression on his face that I was so familiar with from all the photographs, extending his massive hand in my direction. . . .

I couldn't help reaching out for his hand in return, just as I had so many times before in my dreams. But there was nothing there. The Chairman was still lying in his coffin and we inched forward with the rest of the crowd. We moved past the bier which was surrounded by fresh flowers and made our way slowly to the exit.

I bid farewell to Chairman Mao. I bid farewell also to twenty years of my life, the most precious, enthusiastic and impressionable time of my youth.

We walked out into Tiananmen Square which was bathed in bright sunlight. We could see [the portrait of] Chairman Mao on Tiananmen Gate, although Chairman Mao was not there himself.

Even now the songs I most often sing, the songs with which I am most familiar, which I can sing from beginning to end, are songs written in praise of Chairman Mao. The works I can still recite off by heart are Chairman Mao's poems. And I still quote Chairman Mao at the drop of a hat. I know and hold it to be true that Mao Zedong will live on in my heart forever.

This year I'm in Shenzhen for Spring Festival. During the holiday I happened to take taxis a number of times. None of the taxis had the usual talismans for good fortune hanging from their rear-vision mirrors. What hung there instead was Chairman Mao's portrait. I asked the drivers about it and they all said that they hung the Chairman because he could ward off evil.

Dear Chairman Mao, people throughout China miss you.

The Cult of Mao Zedong Persists

Ian Buruma

Mao Zedong was the greatest symbol of the Cultural Revolution. The Red Guards and other revolutionaries proclaimed that they were acting on his behalf, rather than on behalf of China or the Chinese people generally. Activists memorized selections from a collection known as *Quotations from Chairman Mao*, or *Little Red Book*, and sang songs based on his writings. During the years of the Cultural Revolution, statues and posters of Mao often replaced those of other great figures from Chinese history. Indeed, he came to be at the center of an almost religious cult. Interestingly, this cult has not only lasted, it has grown more entrenched. In the following article first published in 2001, journalist and author Ian Buruma examines the cult of Mao. He claims that it is most obvious among poor people and argues that, as the years have passed, Mao has risen to join other transformative figures in a culture that has a great reverence for such men. In this way, and despite the fact that the Mao cult sometimes manifests itself in the production of cheap products with Mao's image, the excesses

---

SOURCE. Ian Buruma, "Cult of the Chairman," *Guardian*, March 7, 2001. Copyright © 2001 by Guardian News & Media Ltd. All rights reserved. Reproduced by permission.

of the Cultural Revolution, and other mistakes of Mao's rule, have been forgotten or explained away. Ironically, given the shift to communism and the radical attempt to erase the past during the Cultural Revolution, Mao has become an example of the strength of China's long traditions. Ian Buruma's books include *God's Dust*, *A Long Asian Journey*, and *Bad Elements: Chinese Rebels from Los Angeles to Beijing*.

A miracle happened in Shaoshan, birthplace of Mao Zedong, on December 20, 1993. President Jiang Zemin had come with an entourage of party grandees to unveil a 6 metre-high bronze statue of the late Chairman Mao, looking, as the guidebook has it, "firm and steady, and glowing with health". Anyone who sees it, the book continues, "can feel the magnetic power of a great leader, a victorious leader". December in Hunan province is a cold, dark month, with constant rain or sleet. The freezing winds won't let up until the spring. But on that miraculous occasion, just as President Jiang was pulling the sheet off Mao's shining face, the sun came blazing through the clouds and, even stranger, the moon shone brightly.

Mao Keepsakes

I was shown photographs of the miracle when I visited Shaoshan recently, on a typically bleak, rainy day. You could buy the picture in all sizes, the most expensive ones framed in gold. You could also buy gold or marble busts of the chairman, tapes of his speeches, fine embroideries of his countenance, and coins, stamps, ballpoints, pencils, cigarette lighters, key rings, CDs, T-shirts and teacups, all with Mao's image on [them]. Then there were the plastic domes with Mao inside that rained gold flakes when you shook them. And the golden amulets to bring good health and fortune with—instead of the more usual images of Buddhist or Taoist holy men—engraved portraits of the former Chinese leader.

Mao Zedong has clearly entered the pantheon of Chinese folk deities, along with the Yellow Emperor and other legendary sages and heroes in Chinese history. And Shaoshan, visited by millions over the years, is the Lourdes[1] of his cult.

This is not so strange. Humans have been worshipped as gods for thousands of years in China, and the point of Mao, in the eyes of the believers, is no longer whether he was good or bad; such categories do not apply to godmen. The point, as a taxi driver in Hunan pointed out to me when I asked him about the Mao charm dangling from his rearview mirror, is that Mao was Great, or *weida*. Great-

> "Mao's divine status has brought a great deal of business."

ness, in the sense of projecting great personal power, is much admired among the Chinese peoples; think of the continuing popularity of [Adolf Hitler's] *Mein Kampf* in Taiwan.

A godman in China or Japan can still have entirely human characteristics—more so, perhaps, than Jesus Christ, whose status with some Chinese is somewhat similar to Mao's. In Changsha, the capital of Hunan, where Mao went to school and founded the regional communist party, I visited the provincial museum, where there is a lavish display of Mao's underwear. That is the interesting thing about godmen: they are both divine and very human.

Divine beings in every society promise salvation and good fortune, and where there are miracles, there is business to be done. This, too, is universal. Mao's divine status has brought a great deal of business to Shaoshan. Indeed, it has become the main cottage industry of this small but prosperous town. Restaurants offer "Mao's favourite dishes". Snake-oil salesmen sell miracle cures for all kinds of diseases. And almost every shop is a purveyor of Mao memorabilia.

Shaoshan, as a pilgrimage site, is surprisingly traditional. Not only does it have all the characteristics of Chinese folk religion, which Mao affected to despise, but of higher Chinese culture as well; for example, the ubiquitous presence of Mao's calligraphy and poetry. One of the tasks of great Chinese leaders is to carry on Chinese civilisation, and the core of that civilisation is the word, which finds its highest expression in calligraphy. No matter how much tradition Mao and his followers smashed—and they smashed a great deal—he kept the word. And so did his successors. Not only is Mao's own rather wild calligraphy everywhere to be seen in Shaoshan—on paper, on rocks, on walls, on silk—but also that of [former president] Deng Xiaoping and Jiang Zemin. Shaoshan, the birthplace of the greatest wrecker of Chinese tradition, has become, in many ways, a repository of it.

There is, none the less, something curious about the cult of Mao, which began in the 80s, roughly 10 years after the Great Helmsman's death. First of all, folk cults are usually suppressed by a nominally communist government which officially, in good Marxist fashion, dismisses all religion as superstition. Government approved, so-called patriotic churches, subservient to the party, are tolerated, but spontaneous cults are viewed with deep suspicion. Secondly, memories of the famines and mass murders associated with the Mao years have not faded away, even though younger generations often know little or nothing about them.

Adjusting the Memory of Mao

However, the bad memories—the bloody purges, the violent anarchy of the Cultural Revolution—are officially classified as "mistakes", committed when Mao was old and no longer in control of his evil courtiers. His alleged greatness—the reason for his divinity and the thing admired by the Hunanese taxi driver—is something very traditional. Mao is supposed to have created order in the Chinese empire by kicking out the barbarians, punishing evil-doers, and restoring virtue. His great achievement in the eyes of his admirers is moral, more than political. Or rather, politics and morality come to the same thing. As the Confucian phrase goes: "Only the virtuous can rule all under Heaven." Mao's revolution, so it is believed, brought back harmony and virtue were there had been chaos and corruption. And, like all peasant messiahs, Mao promised a society in which all men would be equal.

The deification of Mao happened just as Deng Xiaoping's economic reforms once again made chaos, inequality and corruption visible in China. Deng's reforms also meant a restoration of a different kind. Intellectuals, persecuted horribly under Mao, came back as advisers to the reformist rulers. They were the modern mandarins, as it were, at the court of Deng. Tired of Utopian campaigns, they knew that a degree of inequality and corruption was an inevitable side-effect of China's rush towards economic modernisation. But these side-effects can become intolerable if political freedom fails to match economic liberties. That is what produced the protests on Tiananmen Square in 1989. It is also what produced the banned Falun Gong sect—and the cult of Mao.

A professor of history in Changsha, who supports the economic reforms and is afraid of cults and popular rebellions, told me: "The more intellectuals hate Mao, the more the poor people like him." Mao's admirers think that he stood for egalitarianism and righteousness, whereas the current elite looks greedy, corrupt and contemptuous of the lower classes.

Maoism was, in fact, a lethal mixture of Stalinism and Chinese authoritarianism. Like Chinese autocrats before him, he believed that obedience had to be enforced and that social harmony is a matter of imposing "correct thinking", not of finding peaceful solutions to inevitable conflicts of interests. The moral dogma to be imposed can be Confucianism or Marxism, or Maoism, or Communism with Chinese Characteristics. Whatever the dogma, opposition to it is not just wrong, it is immoral. When class enemies are wiped out, there will be no more conflicts. And those who still claim personal interests are evil, and have to be wiped out too.

> Whenever conflicts come to the boil . . . the government falls back on that old Maoist mixture of dogma and tradition.

Economic liberalism, towards which China has been moving in the past 20 years, is all about interests. Businessmen in the rich coastal cities do not necessarily have the same interests as farmers in Hunan, or factory workers in the industrial northeast. And academics and party cadres might have different interests altogether. Many Chinese are well aware of this, but the one-party communist system has no mechanisms to solve these conflicts: without party politics, a free press, and elected political representation, such conflicts cannot be solved.

Mao and Mythmaking

So whenever conflicts come to the boil—students or Falun Gong supporters demonstrating in Beijing, farmers rioting in the countryside, academics writing critical articles on the internet, or workers protesting against factory closures—the government falls back on that old Maoist mixture of dogma and tradition. People are told to cultivate correct thinking, to redouble their studies of Marxism-Leninism, to strengthen China, and to struggle against foreign imperialists and class enemies.

Perversely, the same intellectuals and businessmen who support China's economic reforms are often as fearful of political reforms as the party leaders. They may hate communist propaganda, but they tend to associate multi-party politics with disorder, selfishness, and mob rule. And so, in the name of economic development and

stability, they endorse authoritarian measures to control protesters.

What they often fail to see is that cults are a direct result of blocked politics. Just as autocratic Chinese governments have always justified their monopoly of power by claiming superior virtue, peasant rebellions and religious protests have done the same thing. They were the virtuous rebels who rose in the name of all kinds of folk gurus and deities, including Mao Zedong, to fight corrupt officials and evil rulers, and restore morality. This is why the government is now so spooked by Falun Gong and the many "underground" Christian cults: they offer alternative dogmas which undermine the rulers' already shaky claims to superior virtue.

There is no evidence that any of the cults in China are about to explode in violent rebellion. Most believers, like the pilgrims in Shaoshan, hope for good health, good fortune, or just a good time. But there is much

The continued cult-like following of Mao Zedong was still evident in 2006, when people lined up at his mausoleum on the thirtieth anniversary of his death. **(AP Photo.)**

resentment over betrayed loyalties and dashed illusions. Like the neo-Maoists, many Falun Gong believers were once fervent communists who believed that a new moral Chinese utopia was at hand. The spectacle of party hacks and gangsters helping themselves to riches, while others languish in the margins, has bred a great deal of anger.

There are democratic institutions to contain such anger. But without the freedom to build such institutions, the Chinese are reduced once again to waiting for the next Mao, or violent messiah.

Note

1. Lourdes is a small town in France known for apparitions of the Virgin Mary. Millions of pilgrims and tourists visit Lourdes every year.

China's Leaders Worry About the Cult of Mao

George Wehrfritz

Although communism is officially an atheist ideology, religious traditions have proven hard to repress for long, and as China's economy has opened up over the last thirty years, religion, in many forms, has become more acceptable as well. The Chinese often worship local or favorite gods or buddhas in personal ceremonies involving the giving of offerings, the burning of incense, and a form of bowing known as the kowtow. China is also full of religious sites such as mountains or temples to which believers often make long pilgrimages. The following article, published in 1996 in an American weekly news magazine, reports on how such practices are increasingly being directed toward Mao Zedong, the figure at the heart of the Cultural Revolution. Communist party officials, the article notes, disapprove. They would rather Mao be respected as a politician who helped to guide China's masses rather than worshipped as an icon.

SOURCE. George Wehrfritz, "Mao Was the Best Emperor of All Time: Why Does Beijing Still Fear the Revolution?" *Newsweek*, vol. 127, no. 19, May 6, 1996, p. 44. Copyright © 1996 by Newsweek. All rights reserved. Reproduced by permission.

The 1,200 villagers of Gushuicun live in the cradle of Chinese civilization. Yet they seem to have lost their historical perspective. On a sacred hill in northern Shaanxi province, near Taoist shrines and a traditional fertility hall, they have built a temple to Mao Zedong. It draws a steady stream of Communist Party officials and other worshipers. They light incense, burn paper money and kowtow before a 10-foot-tall plaster likeness of the Great Helmsman. "In my mind, Chairman Mao was the best emperor of all time," says Wu Xuji, 64, the village's energetic party secretary. "We want to worship him generation after generation."

Villagers concede his "mistakes"—the politically correct term for the famines and massive violence he caused—but they prefer to remember the "good things." He was one of them, he inspired them and spoke for them. Most of all, he knew how to tap their immense power. Perhaps that is why today's leaders in Beijing still fear Mao. Thirty years ago he ignited his most violent campaign of all, the Great Proletarian Cultural Revolution. The ensuing decade of chaos provided the negative inspiration for Deng Xiaoping's reforms. Deng and others who were persecuted during the Cultural Revolution now wear their scars as a badge of honor. But China's new leaders have prohibited any serious attempt to come to terms with the upheaval itself.

The Beginnings of the Cultural Revolution

The Cultural Revolution began with a power struggle. Mao's leadership had been challenged by the Communist Party Congress; in May 1966 he struck back. He attacked moderates for lacking revolutionary zeal, then targeted his rivals in the leadership. He called on millions of patriotic youths to form the Red Guards, "bombard the headquarters" of government and dislodge his opponents. What followed was a reign of terror. Marauding Red Guards hunted down "class enemies," smashed Buddhist temples and other so-called symbols of feudalism and effectively paralyzed China's government. The country sank close to civil war—and worse. Some Red Guards units engaged in ritual cannibalism. The bouts of violence faded away only after Mao died in September 1976.

> Party scholars concluded in 1981 that Mao committed 'gross mistakes' that brought China to the brink of ruin.

Party scholars concluded in 1981 that Mao committed "gross mistakes" that brought China to the brink of ruin. But the official verdict also hailed Mao as a hero whose record was "70 percent positive." Future scholars had to walk a narrow line. They could publicize their personal suffering, but any study of the Cultural Revolution's deeper causes was taboo. Today, scholarship remains in limbo. Even anecdotal research stops at the doors of the party: scholars are barred from a vast communist archive, apparently for fear that scrutiny would reveal the party's central role in the horrors.

Remnants of Mao

What are China's leaders so afraid of? Seven years ago students occupied Tiananmen Square, trying to incite political change. To a Beijing leader, many Tiananmen battle cries—"Oppose official corruption! Clean up government!"—can only sound scarily like the slogans Mao used to send students into the streets a generation ago. Could something like the Cultural Revolution ever happen again? Artist Feng Jicai finds echoes of the past in everything from his countrymen's lack of respect for laws to renewed idol worship in the countryside. Others worry about a return of political upheaval: Beijing's neoconservatives play on Maoist issues like the income gap between rich and poor, rampant corruption and the excesses of the new rich. Many survivors of the revolu-

Photo on following pages: Visitors in Shaoshan, the birthplace of Mao Zedong, bow in respect to his memorial. (Justin Guariglia/Getty Images.)

tion worry that young people will never learn from the past. The children of killers and victims alike now attend schools in which the disaster merits barely one page of a textbook.

Scholars at universities across China have requested approval for symposiums or other events to mark the Cultural Revolution. They were reportedly advised—or ordered—to refrain. Instead, state propagandists are urging scholars to focus on another date—the 60th anniversary of the end of the communists' heroic Long March. In that episode, Chairman Mao led his rebels in a retreat across southwest China to Yanan. They survived to win their revolution in 1949. The commemoration, a Chinese editor said, "will dramatize the need for patriotism."

The people of Gushuicun will welcome the celebration. The village was a communist outpost during Mao's 13 years in Yanan. Perhaps that is why Gushuicun's peasants worship Mao. Or perhaps their collective memory has failed. Whatever the reason, the Cultural Revolution haunts them still.

The Cultural Revolution Helped to Expand Educational Opportunities

Arthur W. Galston with Jean S. Savage

The following selection was written by an American professor who made visits to China in 1971 and 1972, years when the Cultural Revolution was winding down. Among the places he visited was a school in Shanghai known as the Ching An Children's Palace. His observations, written with the help of colleague Jean Savage, provide unique insights into the state of Chinese education in the wake of the Cultural Revolution. During the most intense years of the Cultural Revolution, from 1966 to 1969, schools barely functioned and universities were shut down. But one of the legacies of those years was the understanding that education needed to be made available to all, even to rural peasants. The author's

SOURCE. Arthur W. Galston with Jean S. Savage, "The Masses Go to School," *Daily Life in People's China*. New York: Thomas Y. Crowell Company, 1973, pp. 163–164, 166–167, 169, 171–172, 175–177, 179. Copyright © 1973 by Arthur Galston. All rights reserved. Reproduced by permission of HarperCollins Publishers.

observations on the content of education indicate that the focus of this education was on group activity and practical skills rather than on earning high grades. He also notes how enthusiastic the students at Ching An were. He recognizes, however, that the students, aged nine through thirteen, were selected for their special abilities and that Ching An itself was probably a sort of "showpiece" and therefore not necessarily typical of Chinese schools. Dr. Arthur W. Galston was a professor of biology at Yale University.

China continues to be a society in flux. According to many competent observers, and even Premier Chou En-lai [Zhou Enlai], the Cultural Revolution, impetus for much of the present upheaval, is not yet concluded but merely at a plateau—a statement certainly borne out in the remarkable changes that occurred during the few months between my 1971 and 1972 visits.

The philosophy underlying such changes in modern China's educational system is epitomized in several directives, culled from the writings of Chairman Mao Tse-tung [Mao Zedong]. Here they are in official English translation by Peking's Foreign Languages Press:

1. Education must serve proletarian politics and be combined with productive labor.

2. Our educational policy must enable everyone who receives an education to develop morally, intellectually, and physically and become a worker with socialist consciousness and culture.

3. While the main task of the students is to study . . . they should not only learn book knowledge, they should learn industrial production, agricultural production, and military affairs. They should also criticize and repudiate the bourgeoisie.

4. It is still necessary to have universities. . . . However, it is essential to shorten the length of schooling, revolutionize education, put proletarian politics in

command. . . . Students should be selected from among workers and peasants with practical experience, and they should return to production after a few years' study.

5. Besides meeting the needs of teaching and scientific research, all laboratories and affiliated workshops of engineering colleges which can undertake production tasks should do so to the best of their capability.

6. To accomplish the proletarian revolution in education . . . the workers' propaganda teams [and People's Liberation Army] should stay permanently in the schools and colleges, take part in all the tasks of struggle-criticism-transformation there, and lead these institutions. In the countryside, schools and colleges should be managed by the poor and lower-middle peasants, the most reliable ally of the working class.

What could be clearer? The educational system of China, available to all, irrespective of class or work background, and compulsory for all children until approximately age sixteen, is designed to produce "the new socialist man," educated in order to better serve his people and country. All knowledge is to be directed to serving the people's needs; in fact, the distinction between students and workers is to be abolished in the formal sense. "Putting politics in command" means that political considerations permeate the educational experience from earliest childhood to the last year in school and on throughout a lifetime and that the dispassionate assessment of conflicting theories will be abandoned—in short, a positive contradiction of the Western educational ideals of the training of thinkers and the pursuit of knowledge for its own sake. . . .

Translated into current practice, the effect of Maoist theory and the Cultural Revolution is that from the moment of birth, the average Chinese child experiences socializing influences unknown to most Western children. The first stage is the crèche, or nursing room, a service to be found in all factories and most communes. Here working mothers deposit their babies each day and, from this time forward, these children are constantly members of a group. Their surroundings are sanitary and commodious—plain walls, curtainless windows, bare floors, and little furniture. Their physical needs are attended to carefully by trained workers in identical white uniforms whose patience and affection is extended equally to all the children. They spend their days sleeping or simply vegetating in cribs lined up in rows across the room. When they are old enough to walk, they take their meals, go outside to play, and receive their toilet training at scheduled times all together. They are provided with few, if any, toys. In some nurseries, mothers visit their children for a short period each day.

> At an age when many Western children are . . . deprived of regular peer companionship, Chinese children are being guided into experiences that teach concern for their fellows.

In the nursery schools, which engage the lives of young Chinese from about two and a half to six years of age, training emphasis advances from the sense of group to mutual aid. At an age when many Western children are still at home, deprived of regular peer companionship, Chinese children are being guided into experiences that teach concern for their fellows. They learn to button not only their own but other's clothing. Their toys tend toward functionality. Hence toddlers learn to plant seeds and pull weeds in shared garden plots. They take turns pulling each other in little wagons. In the sandpile they gravely pass the shovels back and forth; throwing sand is unheard of. When their groups take walks, each child holds another's hand, not entirely because such conduct facilitates control, but partly because they are being taught concern for the other's welfare. . . .

Both the curriculum and the students' behavior are strictly organized and completely controlled by central authorities. It reminds me of the regimented educational practice to which I was exposed as a child in the 1920s, which I remember still with distaste. Yet the Chinese students seem not to question it. They manifest only strong determination to become educated and trained and thereby to "serve the people." Education, traditionally denied their parents and grandparents, is finally miraculously available to them. There are no boundaries limiting that training, so long as the people do not question the system. And the system has provided such continuing improvement in the lives of the people that even the students, whose Western counterparts are the most visible questioners, have no desire to oppose it.

> Education, traditionally denied their parents and grandparents, is finally miraculously available to [Chinese children].

Drawing a Comparison to the West

A description of one institution that my wife, daughter, and I visited will perhaps illuminate particularly well a comparison of the Chinese and American educational systems. The Ching An Children's Palace in Shanghai is one of several similar institutions organized to give extracurricular training to exceptionally meritorious students, who have been selected for the honor by their teachers and fellow students. We spent an afternoon there visiting classes for children of about nine to eleven years old, from the primary school system, although a few were slightly older—about thirteen—and might have been from lower-middle school.

Quite appropriately, the Palace is situated on the grounds of a magnificent nineteenth-century estate, formerly the property of a Western capitalist and confiscated by the People's Republic for its present use. Our guides, enthusiastic, efficient students, met us with

> Activity—intense, constant, tightly structured—is the watch-word at the Children's Palace.

the inevitable handclapping at the gates and conducted us to the main building, the mansion itself, and, past nooks and crannies, into the countless classrooms supplied by its Victorian architecture. Two interpreters moved at our elbows throughout the tour, aspirating a running commentary in perfect English, supposedly a translation of the strident remarks of our guides.

Activity—intense, constant, tightly structured—is the watchword at the Children's Palace. The two thousand special students are trained intensively in carpentry, painting, model-building, weaving, singing, dancing, instrumental music, and recitation. Our guides determined that our pace should match that of the glutted schedule of their school and hurried us from class to class, allowing no opportunity for reflection or a second glance.

In the painting class, the boys were at one table, the girls at another; bent in concentration over their pictures, they were neatly filling in marked areas with preselected colors. There was no free drawing, finger painting, or clay modeling. In carpentry we watched these specially chosen youngsters assemble precut models, wielding hammers, saws, and glue with awesome dexterity. But no one was constructing a simple gift or a creative form of any kind. Their dancing instruction resembled precision drill. They made few mistakes, and there was no improvisation.

The crowded passageways, the rush, the high noise level created an atmosphere of constant din that climaxed in the orchestra rehearsal room. Again, drill it was, but in this case sheer volume overpowered cadence. Oddly, in the midst of a crashing rendition of a Revolutionary drama tune, we noticed at least one student whose enthusiasm had palled; a little fellow playing a kind of bass viol [similar to a stringed bass] stared into space in utter boredom at another performance. Yet, on the whole, the children were zealous and cheerful; they seemed to thrive on close supervision and crowded schedules.

In one classroom we were astounded to find some of these nine- to eleven-year-olds practicing acupuncture on each other. They had obviously been drilled in the location of effective acupuncture points in the arms and legs. They confidently sterilized needles and inserted them in the proper points. The acting patients reacted with a slight twitch or a quick "o-o-oh" when the proper tingling sensation indicated that the needle had found its mark. None of them seemed fearful of the experience, and, indeed, all engaged in it willingly. Such practice would also seem to prepare the youngsters for stoic acceptance of pain in a future medical emergency.

Different Kinds of Tasks

Following our inspection of the various activities inside the main building, we were taken outside to observe groups of children working in garden plots and running an obstacle course. In the latter exercise, the children demonstrated great agility and fearlessness. They hurdled and dodged around obstacles; they balanced easily across tightropes and narrow planks; they slithered on their bellies under barbed wire. The course undoubtedly develops good coordination and strong bodies, but its implications for training in military discipline were all too obvious.

Returning to the building, we entered a large ballroom of yesteryear, in which folding chairs had been arranged to effect a small auditorium. Seated in the front row with our interpreters right behind us, we were treated to a demonstration of the performing arts. There were others in the audience, students and a few parents, but we were the honored guests. The announcer stared straight out over our heads and fairly bugled the introduction to each number. There were dances, tableaus, a short play, and songs by a chorus. The style in each was derived from the Revolutionary dramas. The dancing, professionally but mechanically executed, gave the children the aspect of puppets on strings. Their youthful voices, in singing and in speech, had been trained to achieve the constricted, hard tone typical of the Chinese opera—brilliant, but lacking in nuance. We applauded their agility and amazing perfection.

By far the greatest emotional impact of the visit came when we returned to the conference room for tea and refreshments. Seated at a long table facing about twenty persons, we were encouraged to ask questions of the group, which included not only the RC [revolutionary cadre or party official] but also certain selected students—the cream of the cream, as it were. At each of our questions, hands flew up, youngsters jumped to their feet, all eagerly striving to supply the necessary information. Often, when more than one responded, it was necessary to restrain the others so that one of them could in fact answer the question. I have never before seen such enthusiasm for a school exercise. Furthermore, their answers were delivered in such loud, stentorian tones that we wanted to cover our ears. Chinese classroom procedure everywhere demands that recitations be sung out loud and clear, and the practice reaches its peak at the Children's Palace.

The children told us that their days start at 6:00 A.M. Even before breakfast they are out in the lanes doing exercise drills organized for neighborhood groups by the Young Pioneers or Red Guards to the instructions of a radio broadcast. They spoke glowingly of the routine opening exercises of their regular schooldays—twenty minutes devoted to readings from Chairman Mao, after which the students recount their activities of the previous day. Each one strives to relate his experiences to the teachings of the Chairman and to illustrate how he has bettered himself for service to the people.

Photo on following page: In 1972, a teacher at a secondary school in China gives a lesson in traditional Chinese painting under a portrait of Chairman Mao. (AP Photo.)

On the three days a week they go to Ching An, the children have only four morning classes of forty minutes each—in arithmetic, history, language, and composition. On other days there are five lessons, three in the morning, two in the afternoon, ending at 2:20 in the afternoon, after which there is an hour for "mutual small groups"— special sessions during which slow learners are assisted in their schoolwork under the tutelage of their brighter peers. We were heartened indeed to learn of this remarkable and useful application of Mao's dictums on mutual aid—the first time we had heard of a concession to, or even acknowledgment of, the needs of atypical children.

Students Helping Students

Upon seeing our interest, the students themselves elaborated. No matter how a child is hampered in normal school progress—he may be a slow learner, he may be hyperactive or painfully withdrawn—he is turned over to his more typical classmates for help. Example and persuasion are the approved methods by which he is urged to adopt a behavioral mode that is considered more desirable for the group. The children, and their elders, insisted that such techniques inevitably succeed. It suggested Skinnerian [teachings of psychologist B.F. Skinner] reinforcement: "If you go along with the group," the lesson seems to say, "you will get along and be accepted by your fellows. If, however, you deviate, we will continue to work on you to get you to conform." Judging by the enthusiastic discipline of the models at the Children's Palace, the pressure to conform must be practically irresistible.

They recited other activities with pride. There are opportunities for special military training. Sometimes they report to factories for instruction and work. A young Red Guard volunteered that children in one primary school put together and manufacture such simple items as mosquito nets. The children at another school learned so much about herbal medicine that they were able to treat some of each others' minor illnesses.

The children emphasized that, although final examinations are given in school and grades are received, these are not the main criteria for advancement. Attitude toward the group and morals are more important. Many children, for example, show their cooperative nature by volunteering to help physically handicapped children. Some even constructed a special cart for a lame child and now vie for the responsibility of his daily care.

> Attitude toward the group and morals are more important [than grades].

"But what," my wife asked, "is done for the deeply troubled child—what are the psychological resources for treatment of the truly aberrant?" The question seemed to fall on uncomprehending ears; no one knew how to grapple with it. The briskness faltered. There was another allusion to "mutual small groups." Someone else mentioned that a shy child would be helped by others living in his street or lane to accept responsibility to speak; all agreed that a child with emotional problems would be asked to repeat the sayings of Chairman Mao and, with sympathetic aid from his peers, would gradually gain confidence. No specially trained personnel are required for this therapy.

I asked whether the children giving these remarkably comprehensive answers were representative of their age group or had been chosen because they were especially bright or spoke exceptionally well. A thirteen-year-old replied that all children would react in much the same way, because their training enables them to be confident and secure and to speak in public.

When we departed from Ching An, groups of children lined up and applauded us much as they had when we arrived. We, of course, applauded back. They seemed unsurprised by any aspect of our behavior, in fact, showed no curiosity about us at all. As we got through the gates and were beginning to savor our release from the pounding insistence of the Palace ambience, we heard another burst of applause. They were greeting another group of visitors before we were out of earshot. The impression that these children are constantly on exhibition and, in some sense, showpieces was unavoidable.

Political Conflict Led to the Removal of Chinese Leader Deng Xiaoping

Joshua Kurlantzick

The Cultural Revolution was caused, at least in part, by political conflicts among members of China's ruling elite: the Central Committee of the Communist Party of China. Mao Zedong, who had towered above all others, had lost a bit of his influence as a result of the failures of the economic reforms known as the Great Leap Forward (1958–61), and rivals such as Liu Shaoqi and Lin Biao were growing more prominent and assertive. In the middle was Deng Xiaoping, deputy premier and a talented diplomat. A Mao loyalist, Deng nevertheless preferred free market economic practices to the strict state control of the economy favored by Mao and other top "leftists." The following selection traces Deng Xiaoping's rapid fall from grace in the first stages of the Cultural Revolution to his rise to leadership. As the paramount leader of China, Deng supported reforms in 1979 that helped turn the nation into an economic powerhouse. Although Deng had served for Mao for two decades, in 1966, Mao began attacking Deng for "pursuing the capitalist road." Deng was banished with his wife for "re-education" and forced to perform hard labor. His son, Deng Pufang, was terrorized by Red Guards to the extent that he was forced out of a fourth-floor window and became paralyzed. Only in 1973, with the Cultural Revolution's excesses finally over, was Deng rehabilitated politically. Joshua Kurlantzick is an American journalist and currently a Fellow for Southeast Asia at the Council on Foreign Relations.

D eng Xiaoping frowned upon the cult of Mao and shunned the showy diplomatic games of Communist China's first premier, Zhuo Enlai. Perhaps because of his down-to-earth style and his disinterest in grand ceremony, Deng has attracted few serious biographies outside China. Certainly, Ezra Vogel's encyclopedic *Deng Xiaoping and the Transformation of China* is the most exhaustive English retelling of Deng's life. Vogel, an emeritus professor at Harvard, seems to have interviewed or found the memoirs of nearly every person who spoke with Deng, and has painstakingly re-created a detailed and intimate chronology of Deng's roller-coaster career.

Like most of the first- and second-generation party members who became senior leaders after the Communists prevailed in the Chinese civil war in 1949, Deng had a revolutionary background. He served in the Communist underground in Shanghai and other cities in the 1920s, and then joined the Long March to the party's Shaanxi stronghold, all the while growing close to Mao, who valued Deng's organizational skills and ability to connect to average people with his direct speaking style. In the civil war, Deng served as military leader and political commissar, leading sizable battles and at one point overseeing some half-million men. After the war he served Mao for nearly two decades in the leadership, gaining insight into politics, economics and governing. When he was responsible for the party's relations with communist parties in other nations, he used his connections to bring new technology to China. Deng, who had studied in France in the '20s, also saw that, despite Mao's campaigns of industrialization and collectivization, China was lagging behind other communist states in economic development.

> Whatever revolutionary ideology Deng may have espoused was purged, along with his career, during the Cultural Revolution.

Deng During the Cultural Revolution

But whatever revolutionary ideology Deng may have espoused was purged, along with his career, during the Cultural Revolution. Many top leaders suffered during the Cultural Revolution, in which Mao turned the party against itself in what scholars have called the Chairman's "last revolution," but few could have suffered more than Deng. Always fearful of potential rivals and wary of Deng's inherent pragmatism, which had led Deng to quietly critique some of Mao's most disastrous campaigns, Mao started attacking Deng in 1966 for allegedly "pursuing the capitalist road." Day after day China's state media lashed Deng with criticisms. The next year Mao placed him under house arrest, and in 1969 Deng and his wife, Zhou Lin, were sent to Jiangxi province for "re-education" and forced to perform hard labor.

Red Guards harassed Deng's five children in Beijing, eventually sending them to the countryside and hard labor as well. Vogel explains that before Deng was sent away for re-education, one of his children, 24-year-old Deng Pufang, was treated so harshly by Red Guards that he fell from a high window and broke his spine. (Other sources suggest that Deng's son was defenestrated.) Because Deng had been ostracized politically, doctors at the Beijing hospital refused to perform surgery on his

> Deng never forgot the pain of the Cultural Revolution.

son. Deng Pufang was kept alive, but he remained paralyzed from the chest down; as Vogel notes, when Deng learned of his son's fate, he sat in silence, smoking cigarette after cigarette. Deng would eventually take responsibility for the bathing and care of Deng Pufang.

Deng never forgot the pain of the Cultural Revolution. During his time in the country he reflected on the party's failures, and in later conversations with foreigners, Vogel writes, he would passionately describe the period as a disaster for China. When Mao, aging and sick, restored Deng to Beijing in the early 1970s, Deng was determined that the party overcome its obsession with internal purity and political revolutions, and instead devote itself to implementing China's modernization. The party's legitimacy would rest not only on ideas but also on providing a better life for Chinese citizens. This might seem an obvious idea, but after decades of Mao's perpetual campaigns, and his derision of peasants' lives—Mao famously said that he would sacrifice half of mankind to win a nuclear war—pragmatism and modernization were revolutionary in China. Deng's visits to Japan, Europe and the United States in the mid- and late 1970s, where he witnessed highly automated manufacturing, high-speed trains and other state-of-the-art technology, further convinced him of China's benighted state. Unlike Mao, he was willing to admit that China had fallen behind economically, as even other poor Asian nations like South Korea had begun to take off, and that to modernize, China needed help from abroad and the rule of law (at least in economic areas). In a country just emerging from the Cultural Revolution, during which a tyranny of the mind mocked expertise and punished or crushed those who possessed it, and where leaders had for millenniums believed that China

Deng Xiaoping (center) and Liu Shaoqi (second from left) are seen off at the Beijing airport in July 1963 on their way to a meeting in Moscow with Soviet leaders, before they lost power during the Cultural Revolution. (**AP Photo/ Xinhua.**)

was the center of the world, these, too, were shocking ideas.

Deng as a Leader

Deng had always been a relatively pragmatic person, but his pragmatism became a secular religion as he ascended to the top of the leadership. "Practice is the Sole Criterion for Judging Truth," read one article championed by Deng. Results, not ideology, would determine policies. (Today Chinese students study Deng Xiaoping Theory alongside Mao's life and maxims, but Deng's theories consist mostly of common-sense maxims on governance and economic management.) Following Mao's death in 1976, Deng used his political skills and popularity among senior leaders and the public to outflank Mao's appointed successor, Hua Guofeng, and the Gang of Four. Deng maneuvered Hua into the background but did not have him murdered or jailed, setting the stage for future peaceful transitions.

Nor did Deng try to completely erase his predecessors, as Mao had attempted to banish all of China's traditions, leading to vast cultural devastation. Deng maintained Mao as a father figure of the party, keeping his portrait atop Tiananmen and mostly whitewashing Mao's grievous crimes. Yet he recognized that much of Mao's thinking on political and economic development had been wrong. Deng also removed the poison from the idea of learning from the West and even from hated Japan. When visiting the United States, Deng told his aides that the one place he wanted to see was Wall Street, a symbol of American economic might, the wellspring, more than tanks or aircraft carriers, of US power. "China must catch up with the most advanced countries in the world," he warned. He allowed universities to open again and met with Chinese-American Nobel laureates to understand how China could improve its basic sciences. He oversaw growing state funding of basic research and fostered a new atmosphere of respect for learning. Deng even supported the idea that Chinese graduate students should study abroad, another implicit admission of how far behind China had fallen.

Most important, beginning in the late '70s Deng relaxed economic and social rules, unleashing pent-up entrepreneurship and allowing average people to live their lives without fearing that the party would be lurking in their bedrooms and kitchens. Journals, fiction publishing houses and cinemas were reopened. Foreign investment was welcomed, particularly in the new special economic zones in southern China, where investors were given tax incentives and largely insulated from China's laws, or lack thereof. The government allowed farmers to start selling their crops, began cutting state subsidies and promoted town- and village-level enterprises. Perhaps more significantly, Deng, the most visible figure in China, purportedly said that "to get rich is glorious," signaling that, unlike in previous decades, the state would support capitalists instead of punishing them.

But contrary to the beliefs of many Americans who met Deng, his focus on modernization and his abandonment of radical Maoist social and political engineering did not make him a democrat. After Nixon's breakthrough visit to China in 1972, Washington and Beijing strengthened their relationship; facing a common enemy in Moscow, American policy-makers wanted to see only the best characteristics in their Chinese peers. And upon meeting Deng, they found it easy to think of him as a reformer. He talked in terms that Americans eager to befriend China as an ally could understand, and he used the kind of casual, direct language common to American politicians. In 1978 *Time* named Deng "Man of the Year" for launching China's modernization; Chinese state media, in return, portrayed Deng's 1979 trip to the United States in a positive light, spreading images of American life that helped to inspire Chinese desires for growth, entrepreneurship and Western consumer goods. Deng told an audience at Temple University that he respected the college's commitment to academic freedom; at other stops he praised the openness of American society.

China After Deng

In a country facing such vast challenges, domestically and internationally, it's not at all clear that even Deng, who at times enjoyed the respect of average people as well as the country's most powerful institutions, could have overseen a Chinese transition to democracy. The one top Chinese leader who has the public's respect and also seems committed to liberalization, Premier Wen Jiabao, is an increasingly lonely voice, ignored by many of his colleagues. When he steps down in the next two years, there will be no one with Wen's authority among the public to replace him. Many Chinese officials, who have forgotten Deng's warning that "if one day China should seek to claim hegemony in the world, then the people of the world should . . . fight against it," seem shocked at how badly Beijing has muddled its relations with other countries in the past two years. They are also recognizing how far China actually remains from global leadership.

Deng Xiaoping's Unique Skills Led to His Reentrance into Chinese Politics

Uli Franz

China's transformation to an economy based on production for export and on free market principles was guided by Deng Xiaoping, the leading figure in the nation from 1979 until his death in 1997. But Deng, an old associate of Mao Zedong, had had a difficult time during the Cultural Revolution. At its beginning in 1966, Deng was highly criticized for being too open to a free economy, for taking, as revolutionaries put it, the "capitalist road." He was ousted from political influence and spent several years in exile. The following selection describes Deng's reentrance into China's circles of power in 1973. Mao Zedong in particular, the author notes, had once again grown aware of Deng's unique skills and of the contributions he could make to China's economic and foreign policy.

SOURCE. Uli Franz, "Perilous Tug-of-War," *Deng Xiaoping*. New York: Harcourt Brace Jovanovich, 1988, pp. 225–228. Copyright © 1988 by Harcourt, Inc. All rights reserved. Reproduced by permission.

Deng's position was not secure, and he continued to be opposed by such "leftists" as the so-called Gang of Four, who wanted to continue the Cultural Revolution. But, as the writer explains notes, Deng's rehabilitation was a fact of Chinese politics once Mao recognized his importance once again. Uli Franz is a German author whose books include *China's Holy Mountains* and *Tibet*.

"Isn't that. . . . No, that's not possible!" The puzzled guest was not mistaken. The elderly little man in the caramel-colored "Mao suit" was none other than Deng Xiaoping. His custom-made suit hung poorly on him, nor was his step spritely. In the massive chandelier's cold light, the returnee seemed still stamped by his exile. He stood off to the side as the leadership collective as a group entered the ceremonial lobby of the Peoples' Congress Hall, running straight into the arms, as it were, of their beaming host: Prince Sihanouk [of Cambodia; then known as Campuchea] was giving a state banquet.

Even before the first course had been carried to the circular tables, the illustrious guests, Chinese party functionaries and foreign diplomats, were invited to view some photographs. Just back from his former Khmer empire, the Prince was indicating with a pointer on charts the successes of the Khmer Rouge in the "liberated zones" of Campuchea. Although Deng kept to the sidelines, word of his appearance spread through the group like wildfire. The foreigners reacted with confusion, the Chinese, with astonishment. From the very start of the festivities it was clear that Deng—not the Prince—would become the uncrowned king of the twelfth of April 1973.

A Surprise Appearance

As [Chinese premier] Zhou Enlai began greeting the diplomatic corps of the capital shortly after seven o'clock, Deng still kept apart. This was deemed unacceptable by a certain young woman, taken by unknowledgable foreigners for a lady from protocol. Going up to him, she encouraged him to join the Premier. Her word carried weight, for she was Mao's niece, Wang Hairong, the Deputy Foreign Minister. Deng smiled now. And then hundreds of hands were extended to him, which he shook with mounting enthusiasm.

When Deng sat himself at one of the tables of honor, it was clear he had once more been installed as Zhou Enlai's deputy, as Vice Premier. Who had reinstated him? Surely Zhou Enlai, his old comrade-in-arms, many must have speculated. Seven years later, Deng was to make the disclaimer:

> It wasn't Zhou Enlai; it was Chairman Mao. At that time, Zhou Enlai was gravely ill, and the entire work of government rested on his shoulders. That was why the Chairman recalled me and reinstalled me as Deputy Premier.

If one is to believe his words, the leadership recalled him from banishment for a very simple reason:

> At a certain point in time they thought I could once again make myself useful and therefore they brought me back from the grave. There is the whole mystery.

The ailing, 79-year-old Party Chairman had by then acknowledged that it was no longer a battlefield on which he stood, but a rubble field. Now he strove for unity and stability. Many of the most capable party functionaries were disempowered, imprisoned, or dead. Great names like He Long, Chen Yi, Peng Dehuai, and Liu Shaoqi had been obliterated. Mao had weakened the party during the Cultural Revolution, but had also purged it and brought new energies to it: beside the veterans Zhou Enlai, Zhu De, and Ye Jianying in the leadership now sat Mao's wife, Jiang Qing,

> Mao had weakened the party during the Cultural Revolution, but had also purged it and brought new energies to it.

Deng's Transformations

As of 2011, China has the world's second largest economy, after that of the United States. China's economic growth in recent years has been remarkable, especially given that during the 1960s and 1970s, the decades of the Cultural Revolution, China's economy hardly grew at all and it had remained an extremely poor country.

The beginning of China's rapid growth is generally traced back to the late 1970s and the economic reforms of Deng Xiaoping. Deng had emerged as China's leading politician following the death of Mao Zedong in 1976, outmaneuvering the so-called Gang of Four and other political rivals. As part of his political rise, Deng formally repudiated the Cultural Revolution and further marginalized those who continued to support it. In hopes of avoiding the kind of cult of personality that had enveloped Mao, Deng never took a central post such as premier or head of the Chinese Communist Party, yet he remained the dominant figure in the nation until his death in 1997.

Unlike Mao, Deng was sympathetic to certain free market activities of the sort that had gotten him banished as a "capitalist roader" during the most intense years of the Cultural Revolution. He believed that China should remain open to free enterprise measures as long as they did not go too far and could be reconciled with Communist ideology. For instance, he encouraged localities

the Shanghai propagandist Zhang Chunqiao, and Yao Wenyuan, as well as the factory worker Wang Hongwen.

After Lin Biao's coup attempt, Mao surrounded himself with only a small coterie of dedicated revolutionaries which, however, lacked people of specialized expertise. He could no longer fully burden the shoulders of the most capable among them, for by then it was clear that Zhou Enlai was suffering from incurable cancer. Mao, then, had to look around for a loyal and at the same time capable collaborator. He swallowed his resentment and recalled his old follower with the words:

Comrade Deng Xiaoping has a talent such as one rarely comes across. He has rendered service on the battlefield to seek industries that they themselves found profitable, helping to turn China into an export-based economy, manufacturing products for consumption in the rest of the world and bringing into China valuable foreign exchange funds for continued investment. To encourage further foreign investment, in fact, Deng established a collection of special economic zones in the 1980s and 1990s. In these zones, Chinese companies could work with their foreign counterparts to set up factories and other enterprises, as thousands of American, Japanese, and European firms continue to do in the twenty-first century.

Deng also supported bonuses and other incentives for individual workers, hoping in that way to increase their productivity. Similar reforms were initiated in the countryside where, instead of pooling their efforts in large agricultural communes, farmers could grow what they wanted and sell it on the open market. After the upheaval of the Cultural Revolution, when the accumulation of personal wealth was rejected as a sign of reactionary decadence (and nearly impossible as a practical matter in any case), many Chinese people were ready to take to heart the famous statement attributed to Deng Xiaoping: "To get rich is glorious."

and is an aggressive fighter against Soviet revisionism. In addition, he knows something of economics and military science.

This praise from the mouth of the highest was not intended for the masses, but for Jiang Qing, from whom he had lived estranged the past seven years, as well as for her left-wing hangers-on. These four radicals were dead-set against Deng's return to the leadership, for he was their proven enemy.

Military Leadership

There was another reason Deng was recalled: the Party Chairman used him as a tool to solidify his greatly

> In his well-known style, Deng now rolled up his sleeves and got down to work.

diminished support in the army. Since Lin Piao's death, the leaderless Fourth Army had maintained a wait-and-see posture. Mao could not rely on the First Field Army at all—in fact, it offered opposition because he had brutally eliminated its Commander in Chief, Peng Dehuai. So only the Second and the Third Field Armies were left him. Politcommissar Deng Xiaoping had once commanded the Second, which had evolved from the "Liu-Deng Army." It remained loyal to him. The Third was also loyal, for the Battle of Huaihai they had fought together lived in the memories of the old commanders of both armies. Thus, Mao needed Deng's prestige to draw the influential military men over to his side. Probably, the real reason for Deng's second comeback is to be sought in Mao's loss of military power.

To placate his left-wing partners, Mao did not give Deng any party offices, only government ones. In the wake of the Cultural Revolution, in addition to party committees, ministries and government offices, too, had been debureaucratized. The Council of State, which in 1966 had still comprised ten Deputy Premiers, now had only four. And of these, only one functioned actively in that year, namely Li Xiannian. Mao installed Deng as the fifth Deputy to Zhou Enlai.

In his well-known style, Deng now rolled up his sleeves and got down to work, as in his best years. Through the end of 1973, he appeared publicly on fully 120 occasions. Especially at the reception of foreign guests of state he proved a seasoned, witty, and well-informed interlocutor.

The diplomatic arena had meanwhile become more multilayered and complex, for the Peoples' Republic had turned away from Moscow towards Washington. With the resumption of Chinese-American relations, Deng

Deng Xiaoping (center) and other Communist Party leaders stand at attention beneath the hammer and sickle in 1986. Xiaoping was exiled from politics during the Cultural Revolution. **(AP Photo/ Neal Ulevich.)**

now fought on two fronts: against socialistic imperialism, which was renewing ancient territorial claims, and against U.S. imperialism, which regarded the southern

Chinese island of Taiwan as its unsinkable aircraft carrier. That the Peoples' Republic, dug in for years, now opened a crack in the bamboo curtain is to be credited to the agile, 69-year-old Deng.

The US President's Visit Improved Relations with China

China Daily

When Mao Zedong's Communist Party took over China in 1949, the world was just entering the Cold War, in which capitalist countries such as the United States stood in opposition to Communist powers such as the Soviet Union. As far as the United States was concerned, the rise of communism in China was a great Cold War challenge, and America officially refused to recognize Mao's regime in favor of the now-gone nationalist regime that had fled to Taiwan in 1949. For its part, China had originally tried to maintain a close friendship with the Soviet Union, but that friendship had fallen apart in the early 1960s, and this collapse is generally understood as one of the motivations behind the Cultural Revolution. According to the following article, the instability of the Cultural Revolution ended up being one of the reasons Chinese leaders sought to improve their relationship with the United States in the late 1960s and early 1970s. US leaders gave their Chinese counterparts an opportunity to reenter global affairs. The key sign of this transformation was the visit of US president Richard M. Nixon to China in 1972.

Almost 35 years after U.S. President Richard Nixon startled the world by visiting China, the boldness of the trip and his meeting with Mao Zedong still capture the imagination.

The week-long visit in February 1972 has often been portrayed as a remarkable success that allowed a U.S. president to repair ties with China, put pressure on the Soviet Union and help ease Washington's path out of the Vietnam War.

"This was the week that changed the world," Nixon declared at the end of the visit.

But prominent Canadian historian Margaret Mac-Millan—author of a new book on the event—suggests the Americans gave too much away to Beijing, only achieved mixed results and sowed the seeds for China's formidable economic rise.

The United States had refused to recognize China after 1949, and bilateral ties had been icy for years.

By the end of the 1960s, however, both nations needed each other. A diplomatically isolated and backward China, trying to recover from the disastrous reforms known as the Cultural Revolution, fretted about a possible attack by the neighboring Soviet Union.

> The Chinese desperately needed help to escape . . . the chaos of the Cultural Revolution.

The United States, also worried about Moscow, wanted to boost its position in Asia and hoped China could help persuade North Vietnam to call a halt to hostilities. So Nixon reversed two decades of official policy and went to Beijing.

Although the hour-long talk between Nixon and Mao rarely went beyond generalities, the meeting was hugely significant.

"It was an earthquake in the Cold War landscape and meant the Eastern Bloc no longer stood firm against the West," MacMillan writes in *Nixon in China*.

MacMillan, author of the best-selling book *Paris 1919*, says Washington took a huge risk before Nixon's trip.

As part of a bid to show good faith, national security adviser Henry Kissinger gave China reams of secret U.S. spy data on the Soviet Union.

"They came rather as supplicants to the Chinese and they handed over huge amounts of intelligence and I think they left the Chinese with the impression that really the Americans needed them more than the Chinese needed the Americans," MacMillan told Reuters in an interview.

In truth, the Chinese desperately needed help to escape what China's State Information Minister Cai Wu calls the chaos of the Cultural Revolution.

"Nixon's visit opened a door at that time for China to the rest of the world," he said during a recent visit to Ottawa [the Canadian capital].

Almost hidden among the fanfare, banquets and media frenzy was the joint commitment to boost academic contacts as well as trade—topics which did not interest Kissinger or Nixon.

"The maximum amount of bilateral trade possible between us, even if we make great efforts, is infinitesimal in terms of our total economy," Kissinger told deputy Chinese Foreign Minister Qiao Guanhua.

In reality, the academic visits quickly helped China build up vital knowledge and skills. And the promise of greater access to U.S. markets was crucial.

After Mao died in 1976, his successors launched economic reforms that turned China into the powerhouse that it is now, running a $200 billion trade surplus with

The 1972 meeting of Mao Zedong and US president Richard Nixon is a pivotal moment in China's re-entry to global affairs. (Keystone-France/Gamma-Keystone via Getty Images.)

the United States. China helps keep its rival afloat by buying vast amounts of U.S. debt.

As time passed, other drawbacks of the Nixon visit became clear to Washington. Although the trip did deliver the desired shock to Moscow, it also proved an unpleasant surprise to allies such as Japan.

And despite Nixon's hopes, the China card did not result in effective pressure on North Vietnam to reach a peace deal.

Even without Nixon's visit, she feels, China and the United States would eventually have come to an understanding.

Now, as a confident China seeks to exert its influence and track down sources of raw materials, more problems seem likely with a weakened United States.

"There are areas where they are going to clash more and more. I think commodities are going to be a real problem," said MacMillan.

China's Turn Toward the United States Was the Result of Its Rejection of the Soviet Union

Stanley Karnow

In the following selection, a historian examines the events and developments in both China and the United States that led to improved relations between them. The two countries had largely shunned each other since the Communist takeover in China in 1949. The Chinese, according to the author, had grown particularly concerned with the Communist regime of the Soviet Union. Although both Communist powers had enjoyed good relations throughout the 1950s, their relationship fell apart in the 1960s. Chinese leaders not only rejected the Soviet claim that no Communist nation's policies should differ from their own, they feared the large military buildup taking place along the China-Soviet border in the late 1960s. They also hoped to take on the

SOURCE. Stanley Karnow, "Rejoining the World," *Mao and China: A Legacy of Turmoil.* New York: Penguin Books, 1990, pp. 448–453. Copyright © 1990 by Penguin Books. All rights reserved. Reproduced by permission.

role of a defender of smaller countries against the manipulations of superpowers such as the Soviet Union and the United States. One nation where this role could be tested lay on China's southern border: Vietnam, where the United States was fighting an uncertain, unwieldy war. As Chinese leaders were assured that the United States was going to try to get out of Vietnam, they felt more secure in making or accepting overtures from American leaders, themselves outspoken opponents of the Soviet Union. Stanley Karnow's books include *Vietnam: A History*, *Mao and China: From Revolution to Revolution*, and *In Our Image: America's Empire in the Philippines*, for which he won a Pulitzer Prize.

In Beijing, meanwhile, the conduct of foreign policy had been paralyzed by the Cultural Revolution throughout most of 1967. All of China's forty-six ambassadors abroad except Huang Hua, the envoy to Cairo, had been recalled home for "re-education." On more than one occasion, radicals had physically occupied the Foreign Ministry, destroyed documents, manhandled officials, and harassed Foreign Minister Chen Yi. Chen was said to have lost twenty-seven pounds during his ordeals and Mao, deploring his mistreatment, reportedly commented: "I cannot show him to foreign guests in this condition."

But as the Army accelerated its drive to impose order in China during early 1968, there were indications that Zhou Enlai and his moderate colleagues were edging toward the resumption of normal diplomatic activity. They signed a trade agreement with Ceylon, played host to Nepalese dignitaries, apologized for their earlier troubles with Cambodia, started to repair their damaged ties with Burma, and, in July 1968, granted exit visas to several British diplomats who had been refused permission to return home. Counterpointing these signs of flexibility, however, prominent Beijing radicals like Chen Boda and Jiang Qing sought to subvert the movement toward moderation in China's foreign affairs. They seemed

particularly eager to block efforts aimed at reaching a *détente* with the United States, and their obstruction would make contacts between Beijing and Washington extremely difficult at times.

A US delegation of Ping-Pong players visited the Great Wall of China in 1971. (AFP/ Getty Images.)

Two major developments in 1968 evidently convinced Zhou Enlai and his associates that some kind of *rapprochement* with the United States might be in China's interest. The first of these was the widespread domestic revulsion in the United States against the Vietnam war. This suggested to the Beijing leaders that American forces would sooner or later be withdrawn from Southeast Asia. China could play a role in a peace settlement covering the region. Even more significant to the Chinese was the Soviet invasion of Czechoslovakia and the enunciation of the "Brezhnev doctrine," which asserted Moscow's right to intervene in Communist countries whose policies deviated from Kremlin standards. The Soviet action persuaded the Beijing leaders that the Russians were quite capable of attacking China. The Chinese apparently calculated, therefore, that their defenses could be reinforced by a closer diplomatic relationship with the United States.

In the Chinese view, the Americans had sustained a decisive setback in Vietnam by the middle of 1968. Beijing perceived evidence of this defeat in the antiwar demonstrations then occurring with increasing frequency in the United States, in the popularity of such "doves" as Senators Robert Kennedy and Eugene McCarthy, and in the announcement by President Johnson on March 31 that he would not run for re-election. They were also impressed by Johnson's decision to call a total halt to American air raids north of the seventeenth parallel, an event Beijing noted without its usual adverse comment. The American writer Edgar Snow, who visited China somewhat later, reported being told by a senior Beijing official: "Nixon is getting out of Vietnam."

The same estimate of American policy was indirectly expressed in an authoritative Chinese assessment of the current situation in the Far East. Reviewing the history of the previous two decades, a Beijing analysis accused the United States of having repeatedly tried to "strangle" the Chinese Communist regime. But now, the analysis concluded, the "heavy defeat" suffered by the United States in Vietnam had "seriously upset its deployments for a war of aggression against China and Asia." In short, the Beijing statement implied, the American threat had receded. Now, it was clear, the Russians represented the new danger.

> Now, it was clear, the Russians represented the new danger.

Mao himself was reported to have put his personal imprimatur on the shift in Beijing's foreign policy at a Plenary Session of the Chinese Communist Party Central Committee held in October 1969. Declaring that the Soviet Union had become China's "greatest enemy," he proposed that Beijing seek to establish relations with Western nations that agreed to recognize the Communist claim to sovereignty over Taiwan. As usual, however, Mao's public pronouncement merely served to endorse a strategy that Zhou Enlai and his civilian and military colleagues had already been pursuing for nearly a year.

By 1969, the Soviet build-up along the Chinese frontier had reached huge proportions. Roughly two hundred thousand Soviet troops were deployed in the area facing Manchuria, and an equal number had been transferred to the region adjacent to Xinjiang. Beginning in early 1966, the Kremlin also moved nearly a hundred thousand men into the People's Republic of Mongolia. Outfitted with the latest tanks, aircraft, and nuclear-tipped missiles, the Soviet units were superior in firepower to anything the Chinese could muster. Beijing's forces, stretched from Manchuria through Xinjiang, numbered more than a million men. But in contrast to the Russians, whose contingency plans probably called for strikes against China's nuclear installations and industrial cities, the Chinese were relying on a "defense-in-depth." In the event of war, they hoped to take advantage of their large population to drown an invader in an "ocean of people." Or, as their statement said, making a virtue of necessity:

Ping-Pong Diplomacy

After Mao Zedong's Communist Party of China succeeded in its revolution in 1949, relations between China and the United States came to a virtual halt. The United States was committed to trying to stop the spread of communism anywhere in the world and considered the "loss" of China to be a major blow. The United States and other countries continued to officially recognize as China's leadership the nationalist government of Chiang Kai-shek, which had been ousted by Mao's Communists and had taken refuge on the island of Taiwan. Indeed, Chiang's nationalists, not Mao's Communists, held China's permanent seat on the United Nations Security Council from 1946 until 1971. Communist China, for its part, cultivated close ties to the Soviet Union, its large Communist neighbor and America's great Cold War opponent, in the 1950s.

One of the unexpected changes that took place during the Chinese Cultural Revolution was the thawing of diplomatic relations between China and the United States. This greater openness was the called "Ping-Pong diplomacy," because one of its first steps was an exchange of competitive Ping-Pong players between the two countries in 1971.

In the early 1960s, however, relations between China and the Soviet Union deteriorated as Mao accused Soviet leaders of following a path of "revisionism" in ideology and of trying to dictate to smaller countries and Communist movements. Then, in the later part of the decade, Mao began to seek ways out of the chaos the Cultural Revolution had created. He and other Chinese leaders began to consider opening up to the United States, especially after American leaders made public their

"The outcome of war is decided by the people, not by one or two new types of weapons."

Matching their troop deployments, the Russians escalated their propaganda campaigns against Beijing. Authoritative Soviet commentaries vilified Mao as a "nationalistic anti-Marxist" who had come to dominate China "through the use of violence and unbridled demagogy." A series of Moscow broadcasts beamed to China and manifestly designed to demoralize the Chinese Army stressed the superiority of Soviet weaponry, hope of extricating their country from the unpopular war in Vietnam, China's southern neighbor. Meanwhile, US leaders were happy to exploit a wedge dividing the world's great Communist powers.

The World Table Tennis Championship held in Nagoya, Japan, in April 1971, created an opening. Much to their surprise, members of the US team in Nagoya received an invitation from members of the Chinese team to visit China, a country few Americans had entered at all since 1949. After agreeing to go, and after Mao Zedong and Chinese premier Zhou Enlai gave their permission, the US team entered China from the then-British colony of Hong Kong. They stayed nearly a week, playing Ping-Pong matches and visiting such monuments as the Great Wall of China.

Soon after, US president Richard M. Nixon sent his national security advisor, Henry Kissinger, on a secret visit to China. Nixon himself followed, on an official visit that received much public fanfare in both countries, in February 1972. He met with both Mao and Zhou and, among other subjects, the leaders discussed the status of Taiwan and US support for the nationalist government there (the United States switched its formal recognition to the Chinese Communists in 1979).

For their part, the Chinese National Table Tennis team visited the United States after Nixon's visit. China continues to produce many of the sport's best players.

asserting that "a powerful modern arsenal" rather than Maoist doctrine was the "crucial criteria for victory." The Kremlin also instructed its operatives abroad to contact Chinese Nationalist diplomats and journalists. One Soviet agent, the colorful journalist Victor Louis, even visited Taiwan, where he talked with high Nationalist officials and later wrote accounts of his trip for the American press.

At the same time, the Russians accelerated an ambitious program to strengthen their influence from

Japan through the states of Southeast Asia to India and Pakistan. They sent cultural delegations to the Philippines, signed trade accords with Singapore and Malaysia, reinforced their naval fleet in the Pacific and Indian Oceans, and not long afterward, the Soviet Communist Party Secretary General, Leonid Brezhnev, proposed an Asian "collective security" system that, Moscow spokesmen indicated, would be designed to "contain" Communist China's "hegemonistic pretensions." That proposal, redolent of Dulles's geopolitical pacts, appeared to have been primarily contrived to create psychological havoc in Beijing. For it failed to go far beyond the rhetorical stage.

But the Chinese leaders did register a visible jolt on August 20, 1968, when Soviet and Warsaw Pact troops invaded Czechoslovakia. Until then, the confrontation between Moscow and the Dubček regime had been a real dilemma for the Chinese. They were inclined to sympathize with Dubček as a victim of Soviet "big-power chauvinism," but their fierce hostility to "revisionism" prevented them from openly supporting the Czechoslovak reformers. As a result, they adopted the rather tortuous expedient of assailing the Kremlin for having encouraged the Prague liberals to deviate from orthodox Marxism. Now, however, Moscow's invasion of Czechoslovakia simplified the issue. The Kremlin's "naked armed intervention" highlighted the "grisly fascist features" of the Soviet "renegade clique," Beijing publicists asserted as they compared the Russian action to Hitler's occupation of the Czechoslovak Sudetenland prior to World War II and the American "aggression" in Vietnam.

This response by the Chinese partly reflected their consistent view of themselves as the defenders of small nations against the "super-powers." More profound, though, was Beijing's new fear that the Russians were not above invading China as they had Czechoslovakia. Zhou Enlai openly voiced this fear in a speech on September

30, when he claimed that the Kremlin was "stepping up armed provocations against China while intensifying its aggression and threats against Eastern Europe." He accused the Russians of stationing "massive" troop concentrations in Mongolia and along the border, and added that their aircraft were violating Chinese airspace with increasing frequency. Beijing backed up Zhou's accusation with statistics alleging that Soviet military aircraft flew twenty-nine sorties for purposes of "reconnaissance, harassment, and provocation" over Heilongjiang during a period of twenty-one days in August, and that the Russians had violated the Chinese border more than a hundred times during the previous seven months. Linking these alleged forays to the Soviet thrust into Czechoslovakia, Beijing asserted that these intrusions had been "in no way accidental." Flatly denying the charges, Moscow described them as Beijing's "feeble contribution to the anti-Soviet hysteria unleashed in the imperialist reaction to the events in Czechoslovakia."

> " The Chinese made a move that was to be the start of a wholly new direction in their foreign policy. "

In the face of this growing Soviet threat, the Chinese made a move that was to be the start of a wholly new direction in their foreign policy. On November 26, they issued a formal Foreign Ministry statement proposing that the Sino-American Ambassadorial Talks in Warsaw, which had been repeatedly postponed over the past year, be resumed on February 20, 1969—at a time when the newly elected President, Richard Nixon, "will have been in office for a month" and his Administration had been "able to make up its mind" about China.

The Chinese Foreign Ministry statement was extraordinarily subdued in style and substance compared to the fiery utterances of the Cultural Revolution. At a Warsaw meeting in September 1966, for example, the

Chinese spokesman had demanded that the United States "get out of Asia" and dismissed American desires for "peaceful cooperation" with China as "high-sounding words" that were "not worth a penny." Now, in contrast, Beijing recommended soberly that the United States and China could improve their ties by adhering to the "five principles of peaceful coexistence." Similarly, Liu Shaoqi had been denounced in October 1967 for "advocating national egoism and betraying proletarian international-ism" by suggesting that China could "develop friendly relations" with the United States once American troops were out of Taiwan. Now Beijing put forth that very line, declaring that the United States and China could reach an agreement if Washington merely withdrew its military and naval forces from Taiwan and the Taiwan Strait. Underscoring this policy switch, the Beijing press publicized a 1949 Mao essay which had hailed the value of negotiations and emphasized the advantages of making "temporary concessions" to enemies in order to "win them over to our side or neutralize them politically."

> Chinese Communists perceived that they had fared better with [US] Republicans than with Democrats.

Beijing's policy shift predictably nettled the Kremlin, and Russian commentators were quick to claim that China was "colluding" with the United States against the Soviet Union. Indeed, many of these indictments were minor versions of China's anti-Soviet propaganda. One Moscow broadcast, for example, contended that the "Maoist clique" was "kowtowing to the imperialists and sabotaging national liberation movements" around the world. And others accused the Chinese of servicing American warships in Hong Kong or selling military equipment to the United States for use in Vietnam. Particularly galling to the Kremlin was Beijing's decision to inaugurate contacts with a president whose career had been built on his anti-communism.

But Nixon's record may have been precisely what appealed to the Chinese at that point in time.

As they looked back on their own experience, Chinese Communists perceived that they had fared better with Republicans than with Democrats. After all, they had gone to war in Korea against the Truman Administration, but had signed a truce with President Eisenhower. Kennedy and Johnson had escalated the Vietnam conflict, while Nixon was basing his election campaign on a pledge to wind down the war. Ideology also colored the Chinese analysis of the American political dynamic. Republicans, they believed, were closer to "monopoly capital," the real source of power in the United States, and they were convinced that Nixon, as a representative of the capitalist "ruling class," could operate with an authority that the Democrats lacked. Finally, the Chinese were perhaps gratified to see Nixon's past hostility to the Soviet Union. From their viewpoint, there was a certain reality in the old adage that "the enemy of my enemy is my friend"—or at least an expedient ally.

Suffering for Being Too Revolutionary or Not Revolutionary Enough

Howard W. French

In the following article, an American journalist portrays the contrasting memories of two women whose lives were changed by the Cultural Revolution. One, Wang Rongfen, wrote a letter to Mao Zedong criticizing his tactics during the Cultural Revolution. The other, Nie Yuanzi, was a young university teacher and earnest advocate of Mao's ideas. She was responsible for an influential "big character poster" of the type common during the Cultural Revolution. Both ended up suffering greatly, the author notes, Wang for speaking out in opposition, and Nie for not being doctrinaire enough. The author suggests that, for those who lived through it, memories of the Cultural Revolution are still vivid and troublesome. Howard W. French is a journalist and photographer and a former senior foreign correspondent for the *New York Times*. He is an associate professor at Columbia University's Graduate School of Journalism.

SOURCE. Howard W. French, "The Cultural Revolution: 2 Diverging Paths," *New York Times*, June 9, 2006. Copyright © 2006 by The New York Times. All rights reserved. Reproduced by permission.

The first was an ambitious college professor whose "big character poster," displayed on the grounds of Beijing University, was said to be the spark that set off a prairie fire of violent purges and denunciations, which quickly spread from the campus across the entire nation.

Her opposite number in the history of China's most self-destructive hour, the Cultural Revolution, was a student of German at Beijing's elite Foreign Language Institute. She was selected to attend one of the earliest mass rallies of the period at Tiananmen Square, when the cult of Mao Zedong was being whipped into a frenzy, and all the talk was of class warfare.

The speeches she heard there reminded the unknown student of the language of the Third Reich [Nazi Germany], and she watched horrified over the ensuing weeks, as purged teachers committed suicide, students denounced each other, and her own mother, a struggling shopkeeper, was labeled a member of the bourgeoisie and assigned to forced labor.

"I was transported to the time the Nazis took power," she said.

She gathered her courage to write a fateful document of her own, a signed letter to Chairman Mao asking: "What are you doing? Where are you leading China?"

And it concluded with a judgment that the country's leaders shy from even now. "The Cultural Revolution is not a mass movement," she wrote Mao. "It is one man with a gun manipulating the people."

Inside China, the history shared by these two women has been shunted into a dark corner. There has been no news coverage or public memorials of the catastrophe, in which hundreds of thousands of people were killed and China's economy devastated. Many of today's young who still revere Mao know little about the chaos of the period and nothing of the two women.

The Red Guards parade a suspected antirevolutionary man, forcing him to wear a dunce cap that proclaims he is a "political pickpocket." (AP Photo.)

But four decades to the month after the start of the Cultural Revolution there remains a compelling symmetry to the experiences and reflections of Nie Yuanzi and Wang Rongfen, two women who played striking roles at the outset of this disastrous era, and had their lives derailed as a result.

Imprisoned for Outspoken Objections

However different, in the phrase of Wang Rongfen—then a 20-year-old student, whose pointed letter earned her more than 12 years in prison under a life sentence, which was lifted only after Mao's death in 1976—they were both "bold and straightforward" women.

Nie, then Communist Party secretary of Beijing University's philosophy department, is widely credited with helping start the Cultural Revolution. Now after years in detention, she is an 85-year-old who survives on the charity of friends.

Looking back, she insists she had no idea the poster she constructed would have such terrible consequences. "I didn't know we were heading toward disaster," she said, describing herself as a party loyalist who executed orders. "Once I understood, I stopped following them. I opposed them, and for that I was punished."

> 'Democracy should be really promoted so that each person can express their opinions about state affairs and the work of others.'

Though frail, Nie remains feisty. She recently published a book in Hong Kong about her experiences. She greets visitors with a bright red business card that bears her portrait. And she takes calls on a tiny cellphone every few minutes during days spent at her writing desk.

"The lessons," she said, when asked what she drew from her experience. "Democracy should be really promoted so that each person can express their opinions about state affairs and the work of others," Nie said. "Even if an opinion is not correct, it must be allowed and allowed to be contradicted. Even today, posters should be allowed."

Nie readily acknowledges helping to unleash suffering on others, like the president of Beijing University, the target of her poster.

An Enthusiastic Cultural Revolutionary

He was paraded around the grounds of the university in a dunce cap and sign board, and others labeled reactionaries like him were beaten or tortured by Red Guards, Mao's young vigilantes.

She has spent little time on remorse, though, casting blame on the country's system, where she says it still belongs.

"Back then, we believed the party was great and graceful and correct, and you were obedient to the party," she said. "You went wherever it pointed you."

Once the chaos set in, though, Nie's disenchantment came quickly. At a meeting of party leaders in August 1967, she tried to quit the leadership of the Red Guard, but was refused by Mao's powerful wife, Jiang Qing.

A few months later, she helped avert a gun battle at the university between rival groups and was arrested soon afterward and spent 17 years in detention.

Deprived of a pension until recently, closely monitored and unable to publish in China, she says, the purpose of what remains of her life is to overcome the silence about the darkness that befell her country.

The leadership, she said, has buried the memory of this period, because "it is afraid of losing power. They would prefer for the Cultural Revolution to be forgotten."

Unlike Nie, who insists she was a pawn, Wang, who left the country days after the slaying of demonstrators at Tiananmen Square in 1989, and has lived in Germany since, says she never had doubts about the consequences her fateful letter would have. She simply felt she had no choice but to take a stand.

Wang, who has made a living in Wiesbaden, Germany, as a novelist and bureaucrat, harbors deep remorse, and even today weeps as she describes the suffering her actions brought to the people in her life—from family members to her entire school, which became the target of purges and "struggle sessions" because of her letter.

> The leadership . . . 'is afraid of losing power. They would prefer for the Cultural Revolution to be forgotten.'

A Rare Voice of Dissent

Out of fear of ostracism, exile, beatings, or even death, very few Chinese people spoke out against the Cultural Revolution. Young people especially faced great pressure to participate in the activities of the Red Guards or, at least, not to get in their way. Wang Rongfen, a student of German at a Beijing language institute in 1966, was a rare voice of resistance. After seeing the frenzy of crowds of younger people in Beijing that year and fearing its similarities to Nazi Germany (as she later claimed), Wang wrote a letter addressed to Mao. It resulted in her imprisonment. The letter read:

Dear Chairman Mao Zedong:

I ask you to consider, as a Communist Party member, what are you doing? I ask you in the name of the Party to consider: What is the significance of all that is happening now? I ask you in the name of the Chinese people to consider: Where is it that you are leading China? The Cultural Revolution is not a mass movement; it is one person using a gun to move the masses. I earnestly declare: I hereby withdraw my membership from the Chinese Communist Youth Corps.

Sincerely yours,
Wang Rongfen,
fourth year student of German at Beijing Foreign
    Languages Institute
September 24, 1966

SOURCE. *Wang Rongfen, "Dear Chairman Mao Zedong," Laogai Research Foundation, September 24, 1966. Guancha.org. Copyright © 1966 by Laogia Research Foundation. All rights reserved. Reproduced by permission.*

She plays down her own courage, recounting matter-of-factly how, when it appeared she might be released in 1968 if only she had confessed, she surprised her captors, telling them the paper they offered was not big enough for the confession.

They asked what kind of paper she wanted, and she said "big enough to write a poster," which she would address to Mao, repeating her criticisms.

> 'Poor motherland, what have you become?'

With characteristic modesty, only in a second telephone interview, when asked about it directly, did she speak of her own attempted suicide—she drank four bottles of insecticide on the doorstep of the Soviet Embassy.

The note she bore with her at the time said in part, "Poor motherland, what have you become?"

Though they were on opposite sides of the political struggle and have never met, Wang expressed support for Nie.

"She is a tragic figure who was used by others," she said. "She was hot for a year or two and then lived an inhuman existence for the next decade. I am glad she is alive to tell her story."

Her only venom is for Mao, still revered, and officially deemed to have been a force of good 70 percent of the time.

"I'd say 30 percent good and 70 percent bad," Wang said. "The purges, taking China to the edge of bankruptcy, so many deaths—these are unforgivable. They're not mistakes. They are crimes."

CHAPTER 3

Personal Narratives

A Gifted Student Struggles to Raise His Young Family and Find Work

Sheldon Lou

In the following selection, a scientist recalls the manner in which he left his university training, married, and began a career in the late 1960s, the most intense phase of the Cultural Revolution. He recalls how his wedding itself served as an occasion to praise Chairman Mao and for political debate. The closing of China's universities, meanwhile, meant long years as an inactive graduate student until finally, in 1968, China's leaders declared that it was time for him to graduate and be assigned to a job. However, he writes that, despite his shining academic record, his family background made it difficult for him to find any sort of job at all because of the attitudes engendered by the Cultural Revolution. Sheldon Lou moved to the United States in 1980 and is a profes-

SOURCE. Sheldon Lou, "Wedding," *Sparrows, Bedbugs, and Body Shadows: A Memoir*. Honolulu: University of Hawaii Press, 2005, pp. 202–207. Copyright © 2005 by University of Hawaii Press. All rights reserved. Reproduced by permission.

sor of operations management at California State University, San Marcos.

We had a simple wedding on August 19, 1967, one day after the anniversary of the historic event at Tiananmen Square, when Chairman Mao reviewed millions of ecstatic Red Guards. Kuangyi [the author's fiancée] and I had already celebrated with my mother, grandpa, and grandma at home. So they didn't come to the formal ritual. Yiying, a classmate of ours who also worked in Kuangyi's institute, lent us her room. Friends and colleagues from our university and Kuangyi's institute had been invited to the wedding.

The master of ceremonies, a colleague of Kuangyi's, announced, "The wedding ceremony starts. Stand up. Sing 'The East Turns Red.'"

We all stood and turned to Chairman Mao's portrait on the wall, holding copies of Mao's *Little Red Book* in front of our chests.

"The east turns red . . ." the master sang, and then shouted. "One, two, three, start!" We all began to sing:

> The east turns red.
> The sun rises.
> And China has its leader. Mao Zedong.
> He works for the well-being of the people.
> He is our ultimate savior.

After the song, the wedding master drawled, "The bride and the groom, three deep bows to Chairman Mao's portrait."

We did it. He then announced. "The bride and the groom, three deep bows to each other."

We did that also, and so concluded the wedding ceremony. We distributed candies and cigarettes and

> " Most of the [wedding] presents we received were copies of Chairman Mao's *Little Red Book* and portraits of Mao. "

served tea. A prodigious budget of thirty-six yuans—about half of our combined monthly income—was used to buy those things. Most of the presents we received were copies of Chairman Mao's *Little Red Book* and portraits of Mao, and the largest portrait was from Kuangyi's institute. One thing we could actually use afterward was a small aluminum pot given to us by our Qinghua classmate Yujie.

The conversation quickly turned into a heated debate between the members of 414 [a student group] and the Regiment [of the local People's Liberation Army], because our friends who still remained at Qinghua as instructors or graduate students belonged to one group or the other. As always, each side accused the other of not carrying out Chairman Mao's revolutionary line and of being on the side of the capitalist road-runners. The debate bored Kuangyi's colleagues who belonged to the conservative Nine One Five (915), a mass organization at her institute, established September 15, 1966. Its opposing organization was Nine One Six (916), and it's easy to guess when that group surfaced. Subsequently 414 and 915 formed a coalition as a conservative force, and the Regiment and 916 merged as a radical force. Then the fight between the two coalitions spread through Beijing like a forest fire. But that was to come several months later.

Kuangyi's colleagues wanted to leave, so the wedding master yelled again, "Sing 'Sailing in the Ocean Relies on the Pilot.'"

We all stood again, holding copies of the *Little Red Book* and facing Mao's portrait, and sang:

> Sailing in the ocean relies on the pilot.
> The growth of everything depends on the sun,
> Ample rain makes strong seedlings,
> And revolution pivots on Mao Zedong's thought.

Another round of bows to the portrait of Our Great Leader sent the fellows of 915 off to their apartments and renewed the dispute between those of the 414 and the Regiment.

That was our wedding ceremony.

After the Wedding, A Strange Graduation

In 1968, after we had spent three years as graduate students without taking a single course, our Party finally declared that it was time for us to graduate, without a diploma. That was not bad, really, except that I was not assigned a job. I say "assigned a job" because at that time jobs were always assigned by the university. Students went to whatever place Our Party wanted them to go. It was that simple. But in 1968 we had a big problem: nobody wanted students like me who had "bad" family origins.

Being without a job was not the real problem, however. The real problem was my *hukou*, which was currently at the university. There is no such thing as a *hukou* in the West, so it is difficult for westerners to appreciate how crucial a *hukou* was to a Chinese. A *hukou* was the residence registration of an individual in China and was kept at the local public safety department (the police station). If you had a Beijing *hukou*, you had the right to live in Beijing, and the companies in Beijing could hire you. Otherwise you were an illegal resident and could be thrown out of Beijing by the police. People in the United States still hire undocumented immigrants, although doing so is illegal, but in Beijing no company dared hire anyone without a Beijing *hukou*. The neighborhood committees, consisting mostly of old ladies in the community, kept their vigilant eyes on anyone who looked suspicious.

Furthermore, every single ration coupon—the ones for grain, sugar, pork, beef, eggs, cooking oil, and so on—came with one's *hukou*. So without a *hukou* it was virtually impossible to survive in China.

The dilemma I faced was that no company with the power to get Beijing *hukous* for its workers dared hire me because of my family origin, but without a Beijing *hukou* I couldn't get a job with the smaller companies in Beijing, which might be able to overlook my family origin and hire me. The first company I suggested to the university was my wife's institute. But the institute turned me down. Kuangyi went to see the chief of the personnel department. Getting a job was a more serious matter than a wedding and required approval from higher authority.

Official Approval Denied

The chief shook his head and said, "Xiao Huang [Kuangyi's legal name], we went to Qinghua to review your husband's file. Your husband is excellent, no doubt about it. How many gold medalists does Qinghua turn out each year? Only a handful. He's a one-in-ten-thousand sort of genius. Don't you think I want to hire him for us?"

He paused and shook his head again. "But his family relationship, wow!" he said. "He has uncles who served or are still serving in the National Party's army, air force, intelligence agencies, and every damned place, you name it. I'm sorry, but I'm not in a position to discuss the details with you."

> 'Chairman Mao says everything has two sides, so think of the bright side.'

"But he has never seen those uncles in his life. His father died when he was a little boy, so he grew up with his grandpa," Kuangyi said, trying to reason with him.

"His mother's side is clean, we know that. But, Xiao Huang, this is China, and we have to check his father's side. We're only tools of Our Party, and we've got to strictly carry out its rules. I sympathize with you guys from the bottom of my heart, but there's no way out.

"But don't get upset. Chairman Mao says everything has two sides, so think of the bright side," he added. "You know, after getting the report on Xiao Lou's file, I was puzzled by the approval of your marriage application last year. It didn't seem right. I made some phone calls and found out that they couldn't get access to his file, so instead they checked his mother's. You know that, don't you?"

My wife nodded. She remembered the young man in the department who had made that suggestion last year.

"So consider yourselves extremely lucky—I mean, extremely. You two got married, didn't you? Had we seen his file in Qinghua last year, you two wouldn't be sleeping in the same bed today. Now the raw rice has become cooked rice. We can't do anything to turn it back, can we?"

When Kuangyi stood up and said good-bye, he looked at her and was about to say something. Then he closed his mouth and stared at the documents on his desk.

Finally, when Kuangyi reached the door, he said, "Xiao Huang, you're a lucky girl. You've married a brilliant guy."

When Kuangyi told me his last words, we were moved. In those days people thought Kuangyi had buried her political prospects by marrying a guy with a "bad" family origin and complex "social relationships." Many had advised her against marrying me and had hoped she would change her mind before the marriage. It took guts for a person in that man's position to say those words.

He was absolutely right about our marriage, we had to admit, especially considering the unfortunate lot of many of our friends. We had a friend who had dated his classmate and had made arrangements for their marriage, but his request was turned down by his institute because his fiancée had some questionable relatives. His heart was broken, but he didn't give up. He dated another girl and applied for marriage, but he was turned down again. The third time he carefully selected his fiancée and was sure he would succeed, but the proposal was rejected again by the institute for the same reason. He had no access to the personal file of the girl he had been seeing, and he didn't know what the actual problem was. So he jumped from the third-floor window of his office building. The fall didn't kill him, as he had hoped, but it permanently crippled him. Attempted suicide was a crime, a betrayal to Our Party, so he was also kicked out of the Party. "His political life is dead," as people would say. But I was sure that was the last thing he was worried about.

> The winner of the prestigious gold medal from the most prestigious university in China was now unemployable.

Looking for Work

The night that Kuangyi talked to the chief of the personnel department and returned with the bad news, I cried. That was perhaps the only time Kuangyi has ever seen my tears in our thirty-plus years of marriage. The humiliation was unbearable. The winner of the prestigious gold medal from the most prestigious university in China was now unemployable. Even though it had been clear since the start of the Cultural Revolution that a person with a "bad" family origin was deemed to have no future, when it finally affected me it was still a blow.

That night we lay awake on our wooden bed. We didn't know what to do next.

Kuangyi held my arm and spoke softly, "Don't you worry. I'll follow you anywhere in the world you have to go."

After a few seconds she added, "And our baby will too." She put my hand on her stomach. Tears filled my eyes again.

Soon we had our first baby, a girl with the pet name "Xiao Hong" and the formal name "Yunli," in June 1968. A beautiful girl, everybody said. My sister and her husband were also in Beijing at the time. They helped us a lot in those difficult days.

Yunli brought happiness to all of us, but it couldn't stop our deep concern about my job and *hukou*. It was no use to apply to other large companies or institutes in Beijing, because they all had the same hiring policy. So staying in Beijing with my family seemed less and less possible.

The only comfort I had was that I was not alone. Several fellow graduate students of our department had the same fate.

But I had to have a job. So I started looking at companies outside Beijing. Quickly I found that the job hunting outside Beijing was even more difficult. Believe it or not, there were no employment agencies, no ads in newspapers, no phone books—nothing that would be available in most countries to help someone find a job. So after a while I was desperate.

Finally my saviors came, in the form of two tiny local companies. One was the Inner Mongolia Semiconductor Factory in Huhehaote, Inner Mongolia, and the other was an electrical company in a remote city in western China. Apparently both were also desperate, enough so to express an interest in me and some other Qinghua graduate students.

Mother, Kuangyi, and I carefully checked the map. With only two options, the decision process was simple. Although Inner Mongolia sounded like a foreign country—and many Chinese indeed thought it was— with herdsmen living in yurts, drinking milk tea, and barbecuing whole cows, it was surprisingly closer to Beijing than the city in western China.

That was how I ended up in Huhehaote on September 30, 1968, the eve of the second-largest holiday in China: National Day.

A Young Woman Asserts Happiness Comes from Political Involvement

Louis Barcata

China was almost entirely closed off to foreign visitors during the early years of the Cultural Revolution. One who was able to enter was the Austrian author of the following selection. He made a visit to China in 1966, when few outside observers had any idea what the Cultural Revolution was all about. The selection takes the form of an interview with a twenty-year-old woman, Miss Li. The writer finds that Miss Li is completely devoted to politics and to the ideas and efforts of Chairman Mao Zedong. She shows little interest in a personal life outside of politics. Louis Barcata is the author of *China is Not Following Russia's Footsteps*, *Red Dragon Over Asia*, and *China in the Throes of the Cultural Revolution*.

SOURCE. Louis Barcata, "An Interview with Miss Li of the Red Guards," *China in the Throes of the Cultural Revolution: An Eye Witness Report*. McLean, VA: Hart Publishing Company, 1967, pp. 54–57. Copyright © 1967 by Hart Publishing Company. All rights reserved. Reproduced by permission.

The group showed little interest in the life of the people in the Free World. They asked no questions about how Western women live, about what Western youth is doing. When I made a cautious attempt to find out details of Miss Li's personal life, she raised her head in astonishment about my hesitancy and ventured, "Ask whatever you like. Don't be shy." To begin with, I wanted to learn something about Li's family. She said, "I respect my parents and wish them well."

"Do you love them?"

"Not really. I don't miss them. I am not sad when they don't write to me. Nor do I have the desire to tell them what I am doing and how I am getting along."

"Wouldn't you like to return to your parents if you fell ill?"

"No. I would rather go to a good hospital. Nowhere in China is one better cared for than in a good hospital. After all, at home no one has the time to bother about you. Everyone is working, and they are tired when they get home."

> 'No, no love affairs. Men are not nearly [as] interesting as politics.'

"What about emotional problems? Wouldn't you want to talk them over with your parents?"

"Emotional problems? I have none."

"Have you never failed an exam?"

"Oh yes. It was tough. But in this matter, no one can help me but I myself."

"Have you ever been engaged?"

"No. What for?"

"Don't you want to get married then?"

"Oh yes. Perhaps. Probably. I really don't know. It isn't important at the moment."

"No love affairs?"

She laughed heartily. "No, no love affairs. Men are not nearly so interesting as politics."

"Not even any flirtations?"

She stiffened a bit. "You mean, to smooch around with young men, without letting matters reach their proper conclusion? We don't think about such things. If there are common intellectual and political interests between two people, why should they introduce physical complications that can lead to no good? Or if there is no intellectual basis for a relationship, why should I mess around with a man who only wants to hold my hand and doesn't even know why and for what we live?"

"Do love affairs play no part in the lives of young Chinese people?"

"I believe they do to some extent. There are even a few atypical individuals who consider physical relations important. But this is not the general rule. Here, of course, we can do what we want and act as we wish. There are no social taboos for young people."

Sensitive Subjects

I permitted myself to express some doubts. I asked her where she lived. She said she was quartered in a former Party office, which at the moment was vacant. Did she have a room to herself? Again, she laughed in a certain way, as though she wanted to clap her hands above her head, but felt it would be impolite to do so.

"I believe," she said, serious again, "that at the moment only a very few young people in China have rooms to themselves."

"You have sexually segregated dormitories?"

"Oh yes, if only for practical reasons."

"Are there illegitimate children?"

Miss Li paused to consider. "I think probably now and again. On the other hand, while we were traveling all over the country during the Cultural Revolution, we girls often enough had to spend a night in the same room with a man. Yet, I have rarely heard of incidents."

"Rarely?"

"Well, yes. When millions of people are on the move, there are bound to be a few undisciplined individuals among them. But I doubt that any of them repeated their offense."

"Has anything ever happened to you?"

"No. But my group is particularly effective in indirect, wordless condemnation. Those who do not conform slink away after a few days like mangy dogs."

"By European standards, you are very beautiful, Miss Li. Surely, you must be aware of the fact that you appeal to your male comrades."

Miss Li put down her chopsticks, wiped her mouth with her sleeve, loudly sucked some moisture up her delicate nose, rocked on her chair, and then said calmly, "You see, I am just not interested in this matter. It would only create problems. I am still too young to marry. Once I am ready, I would like most of all to marry a man with whom I can entertain myself seriously the way I am now doing with you. Naturally, I would have children but they would follow."

"You do not hanker after passion, after a great love?"

"My great love is already promised."

"But you have asserted that you had not yet met anyone . . . ?"

Now this long-legged, proud, self-possessed creature, who believed in nothing but the power of the "gray matter" in her head, became shy, like a very young girl.

"Do you love Mao?" I asked in consternation.

"Yes, I do love Mao."

Now, gradually, the blush started to spread from her neck to the roots of her hair. Though she tried to fight it, she did not succeed. I was touched by her. I saw a human being who, although she knew the needs of the human heart, made an enormous intellectual effort to live in accordance with the ideals proclaimed by the men in power.

> 'My group is particularly effective in indirect, wordless condemnation.'

In Mao's China there are millions, dozens of millions of Miss Lis who no longer dream of a young man who might write poems for them, stroll with them in the park, carve hearts in the bark of trees, or defend them against the monsters in the forest. Instead, these Miss Lis dream of a man with whom they can discuss and argue about politics, history, and industrial productivity.

A Former Red Guard Rejects Mao and the Cultural Revolution

Zhai Zhenhua

The following selection was written by a woman, Zhai Zhenhua, who joined the Cultural Revolution's Red Guards as a teenager and, at first, served enthusiastically. She even led groups who beat—at least once to death—adults deemed not "revolutionary" enough. In 1967, however, the author found that her unit of Red Guards was being purged of those thought to be working with "capitalists," and that she was one of those to be purged. Much to her humiliation, she began to suffer some of the same abuses to which she had subjected others as a member of the Red Guards. One of these was "self-criticism," in which the accused were forced to accept charges and insults from others, as well as be ready to criticize themselves publicly. The ordeal turned Zhai against the Cultural Revolution. From a larger perspective, Zhai was the victim of a shift in the emphasis of China's leaders in the late 1960s.

Political leaders were moving away from the excesses of the Red Guards and blind attempts to remake China's culture in favor of returning more power to established organizations such as the People's Liberation Army. After being marginalized following her ritual humiliation, Zhai Zhenhua eventually finished her education as a mechanical engineer and settled in Canada.

When the PLA [People's Liberation Army] team entered our school in early March [1967] they didn't hold any meetings with the Revolutionary Committee or the Red Guards, as I had expected they would. They simply gathered all students in the school together and announced that the Red Guards were accomplices of the working groups in pushing a new capitalist reactionary line. They said that after the working group left, the Red Guards didn't direct their fire at the capitalist reactionary line but at students from bad families. The PLA urged the students to rise up against them. All Red Guards were to make self-criticisms in class and stand again for election.

It was a head-on blow. Like the members of the working groups, I was changed from a leader of the revolution to its target overnight! I never dreamed this could happen to me.

Scene after scene of the Cultural Revolution replayed itself in my mind: puzzling over the meaning of Yingqiu's big-character poster, criticizing the school leaders and teachers, joining the Red Guards and being received by Mao, and raiding homes and fighting the students from bad families. How foolish I had been! I didn't understand the revolution, but strained to catch up and be in its vanguard. Time and again my ability in proletarian politics had been proved wanting, but I never lost heart or gave up trying to improve myself. All because I had such blind faith in Chairman Mao and the party.

Suddenly my faith in Mao and the party centre fell away. I saw all the flaws of the Cultural Revolution: there were no revisionists or capitalist roaders in school, the working group didn't push a capitalist reactionary line, the home raids were nonsense, and fighting the Sons of Bitches was totally insane. If anyone had made a mistake, it was Mao and the party by starting this damnable revolution in the first place. If they hadn't done so, I would still be studying peacefully with my classmates. Instead of bullying them I would be friends with them. Before punishing *us*, why didn't Mao and CPGLCR [Central Party Group to Lead the Cultural Revolution, or Cultural Revolution Group] admit their mistakes and apologize to the Chinese people!

"Suddenly my faith in Mao and the party centre fell away. I saw all the flaws of the Cultural Revolution."

A New Realization

For the first time in my life I wanted to rebel, rebel against the PLA and against this campaign. But I knew it would be useless. Standing on the stage and being denounced by all the students in school was worse than reading a self-criticism in class. Indeed, if worst came to worst, I might even be locked up, like the members of Joint Action [a student opposition group]. Since the Cultural Revolution started our eardrums had been inundated with rebellious slogans, but when one really wanted to rebel one dared not. "To rebel is right!" said Mao. What a load of crap! Only a rebellion he officially endorsed was right!

The campaign went ahead. We spent the first few days studying documents; after that the Red Guards were isolated. The class held meetings without us to cheer our fall and selected five students who would lead the new movement. Two were in my Young Pioneer group before the Cultural Revolution: Guomei, A Lao's daughter, and Jiamei, the class beauty. The other three I knew little about. They were from families of common office staff: Yunyan, Liping, and Xiaohui.

Then the self-criticism started. To keep us in suspense, the group of five didn't make a timetable. They took us one at a time. Two Red Guards went before me. It took three days to complete the process for each of them. They were given time to prepare, and then they read what they had written to the class. In the end they were told that their self-criticisms weren't acceptable.

It was now my turn to write a confession. "When the *duilian* [a revolutionary poem] came out I didn't use my brains to think it over, but followed the current and embraced and preached it. After Chairman Mao had received us, I lost even more of my sense and started assailing students from 'bad families.' Chairman Mao asks, 'Who are our enemies? Who are our friends? This is a question of the first importance for the revolution.' I was politically immature, and in the heat of the complicated class struggle of the Cultural Revolution failed to distinguish who were the friends and the enemies."

These were the main points of my self-criticism. Adding a bit of editorializing here and a snippet of Chairman Mao's quotations there, I dragged it out to one and a half pages. I could easily have made it work better to please my classmates had I said things like "You trusted me and elected me a Red Guard, but I failed to live up to your expectations" and "I deeply regret what I did to you during the Red Terror"; but I didn't. I knew I was wrong, but I had been victimized by Chairman Mao and CPGLCR myself. Besides, I had sunk so deeply into the mire of the lineage theory that I couldn't turn 180 degrees and kowtow to those former "third-class citizens" in just a few days. I needed time.

Self-Criticism

At the meeting the class was set up exactly as it had been before the Cultural Revolution started. I sat in my old seat and read my insipid self-criticism in a low, flat voice. When I finished, the group of five asked me to leave the room and told the rest of the Red Guards to go home. I wandered in the yard but didn't go far in case they wanted me back. My proximity must have been a distraction. Half an hour later they came out and sent me back in alone. The classroom set-up was different. All the desks and chairs had been pushed to the rear, and the front two-thirds of the room was now empty. Looking out of the windows I saw no one in the yard. "Where are they now? Have they left school?" I wondered, but I dared not go outside to look.

After a long time the five leaders came back. I was standing in the centre of the room and they marched towards me until six feet separated us. Yunyan, a girl with full lips, deep eyes, and thin eyebrows, stepped closer and delivered their verdict:

"Your criticism is not satisfactory."

"Why?" I was shocked, although, knowing the result of the previous two cases, I shouldn't have been.

"Because your attitude is not sincere."

They had me there. I wasn't sincere. How could I be when I felt so wronged? Why didn't they try to see things from my viewpoint?

"We want you to write another criticism and read it to the class," Yunyan continued. Her eyes radiated hostility. Behind her the other four stood like a wall. Until then my spite had been mainly towards the policy makers. I now became mad at my classmates as well. In a huff I whirled about and stormed out through the door.

Back home, the more I thought about it, the madder I got. I never bullied Yunyan! I never singled her out or even stopped in front of her during my class inspections! And Guomei! I had even tried to save her

> They wanted me to write another criticism and be sincere, but I would not humiliate myself further. Never.

feelings! If I had told her in front of our classmates what Yingqiu had said about her father—"Who does A Lao think he is!"—she would have cried in humiliation.

They wanted me to write another criticism and be sincere, but I would not humiliate myself further. Never. On an impulse the next morning I went to see Jiaquan, a platoon leader and the PLA representative assigned to my class, although I realized he would hardly side with me. But I had to give it a try. He was the only one who might be able to put a stop to the Group of Five [who were challenging Zhai].

Jiaquan was a small young man with the face of a child, dull eyes, and a flat nose, not good-looking. Nonetheless, he was cool and urbane. As we talked, I sat on the banister against a pillar outside the classroom. He stood upright by another, six feet away, during the whole conversation.

"I cannot do a second self-criticism as required by the Group of Five. I've owned up to all the mistakes I made and have nothing else to say."

"Are you so sure about that? In your self-criticism you didn't even mention the capitalist reactionary line, let alone admit that you had helped to support it."

"I didn't! I'm not a capitalist or a reactionary! And I have nothing to do with their line! I blundered! That's it: I blundered. They don't have to put such a scary label on me," I pouted.

"To say you put forward the capitalist reactionary line doesn't mean you are a capitalist or a reactionary. Don't be confused. You are still a good comrade if you correct your mistake and come back to Chairman Mao's side."

Changing Expectations

"That is if I knew what Chairman Mao's side is! How can I know if nobody bothers to spell it out? Last September, when we were supposedly pushing the capitalist reactionary line, why didn't anyone tell us what we were doing was wrong? One little article in the *People's Daily* would have stopped me, or any of us. As it was, we were exalted to the sky and supported by Chairman Mao himself. Naturally I thought we were on Chairman Mao's side!"

"Perhaps you had reasons. Perhaps there were special conditions when you committed your error. Nevertheless, you did unduly fight your classmates, baffle their initiatives, and cause damage to the Cultural Revolution. I presume you have realized that? Yesterday you recanted to the class. It's a good start. But in your classmates' opinion, for what you did in the past, what you acknowledged is far from enough."

The Red Guards attempted to remake Chinese culture during the Cultural Revolution. (**AP Photo.**)

"My classmates now have opinions! What were they doing last September? They were as quiet as mice! Now that the tide has changed, they all become heroines and jump out to get even with us!"

"Don't hold a grudge against them. They're only trying to carry out Chairman Mao's instructions."

"Indeed, isn't that what we all try to do? It was only because I tried too fervently that I made such an ass of myself!" I felt like crying.

"One can never try too hard to follow Chairman Mao and the party. I know it's not easy for you to go through this, but this capitalist reactionary line must be thoroughly criticized. Otherwise, the Cultural Revolution in schools cannot continue."

"I don't understand. The working group and the capitalist reactionary line were criticized long ago in July and August, and our fight against students from bad families stopped five months earlier. Since then we haven't done anything, bad or good. Why, all of a sudden, should we become obstacles to the revolution now? And why should there be this campaign against us Red Guards? For God's sake, after all we've done for the Cultural Revolution!"

"You seem to be full of grievances."

"You bet I am! If fighting fellow students is a crime, which we Red Guards are accused of, what are our fellow students up to now? Don't you think they are fighting us, and hard? Not only did they fail me, they also failed the two before me. I don't think they'll let any of us pass! Aren't they afraid they'll become followers of the capitalist reactionary line themselves? Then they'll be criticized in the next campaign! You fight me, I fight you back. When will it all end?"

Jiaquan was short of words. How could he know the answers to all these questions? He turned towards the yard and mused, while I stood up from the banister to warm up. It was cold and damp that day, with an early spring rain coming down. Even in my cotton-padded coat I felt chilly. The large stone curb under my feet was wet; so was the brick ground in the yard. Water trickled along the eaves. When the wind passed, fine drops of water were blown on my hands and face. In the patter of rain, I became more worried. So far Jiaquan hadn't given me any sign of encouragement. Would he help? If he didn't, what would I do? Write a second criticism, then a third? No! I must try harder! Maybe I should cry?

It wasn't too difficult to squeeze out a few teardrops. Ostentatiously, I wiped them off and talked with more emotion, voice quivering. "What is over is over. They can't hate me forever! If I have done wrong in the past, it wasn't intentional. I'm from a revolutionary family, and I'm still of the revolutionary masses, not a counter-revolutionary. They don't have a right to treat me like this. I will not do another self-criticism!"

A Leader Demands Unity

Jiaquan gave in. "All right. Don't be so upset. I'll have a word with them and see if they won't change their minds. But you should try harder to make up with your classmates. All you students should unite. After all, you have one common task, to fight the revisionists who are still in power."

I nodded through his words. "Whatever you say," I thought, "so long as I don't have to write another criticism."

> Mao did not mind scratching, bending, or even breaking millions of people.

Jiaquan's efforts worked. The Group of Five withdrew their request for a second criticism from the three Red Guards they had already interviewed and didn't pose it to any of the ones who followed, but that didn't mean we were pardoned. In the next election I failed, with only fifteen votes out of forty. Clearly no one other than the Red Five and the Red Periphery students voted in my favour. Of the eight Red Guards, five were re-elected with a bare majority. Xiaonan wrote a better self-criticism and was re-elected with twenty-one votes, and Ping got the most, twenty-two.

Being ejected from the Red Guards and officially criticized at the age of sixteen had cut me to the heart. So much for my revolutionary aspirations and enthusiasm. In a fit of pique I damned politics, proletarian and capitalist alike, and decided never to get caught up in it again.

From then on I hated the Cultural Revolution. It was nothing but a poorly contrived social experiment Mao Zedong was carrying on, in which all Chinese were his specimens. Improvising as he went, Mao did not mind scratching, bending, or even breaking millions of people. He really cared nothing about human values and dignity.

I hated the revolution for what it had done to me, but I had not yet come to feel a pang of conscience for the harm I had done to others. Like almost all the events of the revolution, in my eyes the home raids were now foolish exercises, and I wished they had never happened. However, the idea of class struggle still held me fast. I still believed that most of the victims of the home raids were bad people, and I had little sympathy for them. I was brought up hating my class enemies and had never heard another side.

Years later, the confiscated goods that survived were returned to their owners, and in 1976, when the Cultural Revolution was over and repudiated, the home raids were cited as examples of human rights violations. I felt nervous, but the many who had taken part in them were not individually denounced or prosecuted.

More years passed. I grew older and was exposed to different ideas. My remorse grew. Despite telling myself that I was only fifteen years old at the time, that I had been pulled into these excesses unwittingly, that it was not my fault, and that I should not have to take responsibility, I realized I had done some very bad things. The victims of the home raids may all have been innocent.

An Educated, Urban Family Adjusts to Life on the Farm

Liang Heng

The following selection provides a personal account of what happened to one family during the Cultural Revolution's "Down to the Countryside" movement. As part of the attempt to instill respect for China's masses of rural peasants, thousands of educated city dwellers were "sent down" to rural areas. There they engaged in the sorts of farming tasks that Chinese peasants had worked at for centuries. Frequently, university students were "sent down" to rural communes where, in addition to their farm work, they spent their evenings in revolutionary education and singing songs based on Mao's *Little Red Book*. By contrast, the subjects of the selection were sent to a rural village rather than a commune. The author, Liang Heng, was fifteen years old when he and his father were "sent down." He describes ways in which his father, a newspaper editor and devoted Communist, tried to transform

SOURCE. Liang Heng and Judith Shapiro, "The Spring Wind of Chairman Mao Thought," *Son of the Revolution*. New York: Alfred A. Knopf, 1983, pp. 176–180. Copyright © 1983 by Alfred A. Knopf. All rights reserved. Reproduced by permission.

himself into a "peasant," and the reactions of some of the local villagers to those efforts. Liang eventually married Judith Shapiro, an American teacher in China, and emigrated to the United States.

The time came for the peasants to teach us. Poor Father. He was totally unaccustomed to labor and made a fool of himself over and over again. In the early spring, the only major work was spreading fertilizer, mostly night soil and the chemicals bought with Father's "investment" [a personal financial contribution]. The mucky pond bottom was another rich resource though, sticky and black with dead fish and plant life. We were supposed to carry our shoulder poles down the dirt steps that had been carved in the bank and go right into the stuff up to our knees. There we'd hook on two baskets loaded with mud and carry them back up and out to the fields, running with that low, even stride which is the only comfortable way to carry an extremely heavy burden. I was strong and learned quickly, but Father never mastered it. I remember him the first day, arriving serious and earnest, his pants rolled up above his knees and his soft feet red with cold, eager to learn from the peasants. But before he made it safely into the muddy slop at the bottom, he slipped on the rounded little steps and flew ingloriously to his destination, bottom first. Everyone laughed, of course, but Guo Lucky Wealth reproved them, saying, "What would you do if you were asked to make speeches like Old Liang? We could beat your asses with a stick three times and wouldn't get a fart out of you." Father smiled good-naturedly. "Never mind," he said. "If I work hard, eventually I'll get it."

After this first fall, he went all the way home to change his pants. He did so again after the second, but after the third he had nothing more to change into and worked as he was, muddy from head to toe, but safe on the pond bottom loading baskets.

A Father Learns About the Life of Peasants

Despite such blunders, Father seemed more at peace with himself and the world than I had ever seen him. He became talkative again, smiled often, and sometimes even hummed under his breath. The exercise was evidently good for him, for he looked younger than he had since before the Cultural Revolution began. He was a little sad though, as he discovered the depth of the peasants' day-to-day misery. Theirs was a poverty he had only touched upon as a reporter; he had been shielded from it by being shep-

> " It was a cruel reality, very different from the one he had envisaged as he read documents and newspapers in the comfort of his office. "

herded from place to place by cadres who treated him as an honored guest. It was a cruel reality, very different from the one he had envisaged as he read documents and newspapers in the comfort of his office. Where was the liberation from suffering the Revolution had advertised so proudly?

Living in the No. 9 Production Team was a shock for me, too, for neither Uncle Hou's nor Cousin Han's Teams had been so poor. The Goose Court Commune had a long history of misery, and in the early 1960s many had died there. The land had been exhausted by years of intensive cultivation and inadequate fertilizers; it grew barely enough rice to feed the Team, but even so the peasants had to turn most of it over to the government. They had a saying that summed up the situation very neatly: "During the first half of the year, we grow rice for the government; during the second half, we wait for emergency relief." Many things made more sense to me now. I understood, for example, that the peasants produced babies the way a chicken produces eggs because their basic food allotment would be increased with each new family member. Then the rice could be redistributed to those who needed it most, the active men. The women and children sacrificed their portions to keep the best laborers fit, and made do with sweet potatoes and sweet potato leaves.

The peasants' only real source of income was the paltry twenty *yuan* they received for each pig they sold to the government. If this money was hoarded carefully for ten years or more, it might conceivably buy someone a bride; even in those days, 300 or 400 *yuan* was a minimum price. In our Team, marriage was out of the question for at least eight of the middle-aged men, and a new house, even one with a straw roof at only 800 *yuan*, hadn't been built for years. The only other money came from the chicken and duck eggs, which sold for 5 *fen* [there are 100 *fen* in 1 *yuan*] apiece at the commune center; with this there might be enough for a little oil or salt. No wonder Cousin Han had rarely cooked with oil!

We didn't have to look beyond our own hosts and neighbors, Guo Lucky Wealth and his wife, for constant reminders of the desperation of these lives. The man's name was a mockery. How embarrassingly splendid our ordinary city furniture suddenly looked! The couple had only an old wardrobe, a rickety table, and a bed that looked like it would collapse at any moment. They slept under a cotton quilt that they had inherited from Old Guo's father; it was black with grease and age, and most of the stuffing had fallen out. Between the two of them, they had only one whole pair of pants, which they shared and reserved for days when one of them went to market in the commune center. As for food, they often put the rice hulls the government issued as pig feed on their own tables, giving their own sweet potato leaves to the pigs. It was not surprising that the government often complained that their pigs were underweight. Every time Old

> " None of this poverty was unusual. "

Guo took a pig to market, he fed it watered-down slop to bloat its belly and plugged its anus with cloth to keep it from losing precious poundage. Even so, officials usually sent it back again. But none of this poverty was unusual. Things in the house across the way had reached such a crisis that the old man in the family, feeling himself too much of a burden, had killed himself the previous summer during planting season, hanging himself from the storage ledge.

There was little opportunity to see better worlds, much less move away from this one. Less than a third of the people had even been to the town only eleven *li* [about three miles] away, and perhaps a tenth had been farther, to the county seat. The only possible means of escape was to become a soldier, the coveted—though temporary—honor given to a few strong young men. Military service took them to Peking [Beijing], Shanghai,

Thousands of people were "sent down" to rural villages or communes to work during the Cultural Revolution. This man is selling cabbages from a commune-allotted plot. (**AP Photo/Neal Ulevich.**)

the border areas . . . and then, when it was over, thrust them cruelly back into their misery. Back at home, they were authorities on everything, but sadly unsatisfied. They looked enviously at the young men coming up who had not yet served, and cursed those still on active duty as "ankle-rubbers"—toadies of the military commanders.

Rural Communism

Father fully expected that officials would criticize his work during the first few weeks, but he was shocked and a bit hurt by Old Dai's complaints. "Other cadres are doing much more than you," asserted the Company leader. "Weren't you told that the peasants were to 'make reports' in the evening as well as 'ask for strength' in the morning? Weren't you told to establish a study room?"

Father shifted unhappily in his seat, and took a hard swallow of hot tea. "But the peasants don't even eat dinner until nine," he said. "They'd be exhausted."

Old Dai looked Father up and down, his red star prominent over his small face. "Chairman Mao teaches us to bear hardship," he replied dryly.

So the next morning after the "asking for strength" ceremonies, Father had the peasants move the sweet potatoes in the storehouse up to the second level. With Zhu Zhi-dao's help, he cut paper "loyalty hearts" for every member of the Production Team and pasted them up on the wall with spaces next to them to record punctuality and participation at meetings. He put up new posters of Mao and Lin [Biao, Communist general], and painted a slogan on every wall. Then he announced that beginning now, according to commune directive, everyone was to attend evening study meetings or their work points would be docked.

To his surprise, the peasants were delighted to come despite the lateness. The storeroom became a center of life for the Team, a forum for working out disputes and making plans. Father read every evening from the newspapers and answered questions about what he read; for people who had never been past the mountain barriers at their doorsteps, it was a rare chance to learn about what lay in the world beyond.

I enjoyed Father's status as teacher, and I had my opportunities to show off as well. I recounted countless times the story of my glimpse of Chairman Mao in Peking, elaborating new details for the pleasure of my rapt audience. Of course, sometimes the peasants asked questions that neither Father nor I could answer, like why Chairman Mao wanted to attack [political rival] Liu Shao-qi. Liu was a long-standing favorite in the countryside because his policies of "more private plots, more free markets, more enterprises with their own responsibility for profits and loss, and quotas fixed on a household basis" had stimulated the economy and made the peasants richer after the natural disasters just after the Great Leap Forward [1958–1961]. But how could we defend him when the whole country was mobilized against him? Still, the discussion was always lively, often ending after midnight. We finished with our "reports," and made three more bows to Mao and Lin, babies awakening and gurgling on their sisters' backs as if they were being given a water buffalo ride.

> "Why wasn't he using every moment of the day to instruct the peasants in Chairman Mao Thought?"

But a few weeks later, Father was told it still wasn't enough. Why wasn't he using every moment of the day to instruct the peasants in Chairman Mao Thought? demanded Old Dai. In the other Teams, the cadres brought their work into the fields. . . .

That evening, in front of more than a hundred pairs of eyes, Father turned to Chairman Mao and said, "I'm sorry, Great Helmsman. I have wronged you. I haven't done enough to bring the spring wind of your Thought to the Number Nine Production Team."

Before he could go on, a chorus of voices interrupted him. "No, Chairman Mao, it's not true. Old Liang is a good man."

"He's made our Team very beautiful, putting up quotations from your work everywhere."

"He's brought us a lot of knowledge and never asks us to feed him or bring him wine to drink like the other cadres."

"He's come from such good surroundings all the way to our poor Team to teach us. . . ."

It wasn't until that moment that I realized how deeply the peasants had taken Father into their hearts.

Life During the Cultural Revolution and Beyond

Chou Linlin, as told to Yarong Jiang and David Ashley

In the following selection a woman describes her experiences during the Cultural Revolution and the ways in which they have affected her in the years since. The selection provides an example, through oral history rather than a written account, of what the Chinese call "scar literature." Scar literature focuses directly on the experiences of those who participated in, and often suffered from, the Cultural Revolution and its uncertain aftermath. Chou Linlin came from a prosperous family, and her father ran a factory in Shanghai before he was "demoted" by workers caught up in the new movement. Her family dispersed during the Cultural Revolution's first years, and she herself was "sent down" to the countryside. After the Revolution ended, Chou's family was reunited and their property returned, and Chou found work at a factory. But she found herself unprepared to cope with the challenges and corruption of China's new, open

SOURCE. Chou Linlin, as told to Yarong Jiang and David Ashley, "Chou Linlin, Female: Former Head of a Factory Clinic," *Mao's Children in the New China: Voices From the Red Guard*. Oxford: Routledge, 2000, pp. 68–74. Copyright © 2000 by Taylor & Francis Books UK. All rights reserved. Reproduced by permission.

economy and the factory eventually shut down. When she told her story, in 2000, Chou continued to face an uncertain future.

I'm so unhappy these days. When Li asked me if I could talk to you I said to myself: Why not? Let people know how miserable I feel. I've nothing to lose and nothing to do at home. I certainly have time to talk to you.

I always knew my place and obeyed all the rules. I was the same as my father. He came from a rich family and was its only heir. My grandfather was a merchant in Ningpo [a coastal region in Zhejiang province] who moved to Shanghai.

Grandfather sent my father to Shanghai Hujiang University for a modern education. But he chose father's wife for him. Mother is uneducated. She never worked outside the house. Her life was centered on husband and children. People from Ningpo tend to abide by custom and tradition. My family was always very conservative.

If a leaf dropped on father's head he'd be scared to death. Before liberation, he had owned a factory that made organic pigment. In the late 1950s, when collectivization started, he handed the business over to the government. So, he became a "Red Capitalist." Actually, in temperament, father is more of an intellectual than a businessman. He was quite happy to swap the ownership of his factory for an "iron bowl" [economic security]. He was, at the time, the leading authority on organic pigment in the Shanghai Bureau of Chemical Industry. Because he had the status of "expert" the government gave him a very high salary.

Before the Cultural Revolution my family lived quite comfortably. We had our own three-floor house. Father's salary, together with our family savings, gave us a higher standard of living than most urban Chinese. We had no worries at all.

Targeted by Cultural Revolutionaries

When the movement began I was just finishing my first year in middle school. I had no idea what was going on. Father spent a lot of time talking with my brothers. I soon realized my family would be in trouble. I felt I was waiting in line to get a shot. All I wanted was for it to be over quickly. I secretly hoped that people would come to raid our house, the sooner the better.

Finally, the Workers' Rebellion Team from my father's factory arrived. It was a rainy day. I remember it distinctly. All five kids were taken to the upstairs spare room. My parents didn't want us to see what was going on. I listened to the raindrops on the roof. None of us talked.

The raid was carried out gently. Father had a reputation as an honest and decent man, and he had had a good relationship with his workers. The workers said they'd organized the raid so that my father would be spared a visit from the Red Guards, which, certainly, would have been a lot worse. Afterwards, they put paper seals on windows and furniture to show everyone that our house had been subjected to "revolutionary action." Luckily for us, this was the only time we had to endure a raid.

> Father was demoted to the rank of worker, and his salary was reduced.

Father was demoted to the rank of worker, and his salary was reduced. He'd never performed manual labor before. It was hard for him, both mentally and physically. Although I wasn't old enough to grasp the big political picture I was aware of the effect this was having on our lives. I stayed home a lot. There were only one or two friends I could talk with. Like me, they had a "black" family background.

Members of a farming commune walk past a Chinese factory building under construction in 1978. After the Cultural Revolution, workers faced an uncertain future in the new open economy. **(Carl Mydans/Time & Life Pictures/Getty Images.)**

One night, one of these friends came to see me. Without saying a word she started to cry. I didn't ask why but just cried too.

All five children in my family were in school when the Cultural Revolution began. My eldest brother was about to graduate from Fudan University. All but the youngest sister went to the countryside between 1968 and 1970. My second brother actually had a chance to stay in Shanghai since the eldest brother was already in the countryside. But he decided to leave so I'd have a good chance of being assigned to Shanghai the following year. He told me that, because he was a boy, he was the one who should go.

However, when I graduated the following year the government's policy had changed. We were told that the class of 1968 would be "Completely Red." Everyone had to go to the countryside. The next year, the same thing happened to my younger sister.

I didn't complain about my poor luck. How could I add to my parents' unhappiness? In any case, I wasn't afraid to go to the countryside. My school had assigned me to a good rice-growing region. So about the only thing I knew about where I was going was that I'd be able to eat rice the year round.

The train—the first I'd taken my entire life—carried me through many strange places. I'd never been out of Shanghai. I was barely 16 years old, with no understanding of peasant life. Yet, I didn't worry at all. Quite mindless, right? Most of us were the same though.

Adjusting to Country Life

There were three other students in my production team. None of us knew how to cook—not even steamed-egg soup. The commune gave us two very small cottages in which to live. They were made of mud, with no chimney. Every time we tried to light a fire we had to run outside in order to escape the thick smoke. I shared the cottage with another girl. My parents had packed everything they thought I might need—from toilet paper to a cutting board. My companion's family had done the same. So it was as if a couple of families had moved in together.

The peasants were very poor. But they were the most generous people I ever met. Often, on rainy days we couldn't start a fire because the kindling was so damp. But, when this happened, the team leader simply invited us to eat at his home or asked other families to send us food. At the beginning, we didn't realize we were getting the best food available.

> We were very silly city kids indeed.

Once, a family cooked us some rice cakes that they'd stored for more than a year. Of course, the cakes were moldy and tasted terrible. We threw them into the rice paddy. A couple of days later some peasants were netting small fish in the field. They caught the rice cakes instead. Before long, the whole village knew about it. Ah! Everyone scolded us for weeks.

We were very silly city kids indeed. I owe those people a great deal for the years I spent in their village. When I received my first month's salary working in Shanghai in 1979 I sent half of it back to the village. Just a small gesture of thanks.

In 1973, the other three students in my production team were allowed to return to Shanghai because they were their parents' only children. The justification was that aged parents needed at least one child to live with them. This kind of opportunity changed my perspective. I'd not been unhappy before. However, now I was left all alone in the village. I was deeply depressed. My family urged me to leave and to return to Shanghai. They thought I'd be unable to cope with the situation.

The village leader was one of those good communist members. He sent his daughter to sleep in my house, just to keep me company. In fact, he treated me as if I were his own child. I appeared at his family's dinner table more frequently than ever. Before long, he decided to make me the "barefoot doctor" for the production brigade. His support was critical in my life. I stayed in the village. But I was unsettled. I missed my family.

By 1972, many universities and local factories were recruiting "sent-down" students from the countryside. Competition for positions created hostility among old friends. Opportunity caused corruption. Things got quite ugly.

Social Status Persists

I didn't try to compete with others. Partly, this was because I was not an aggressive person; also it was because I felt my family background would put me at a disadvantage. In fact, my "bad" family background didn't mean much to the peasants. They said I was from a "high-class category," which made me sound rather superior. I was rather confused by the use of this flattering term. Later, I found out that many peasants insisted on calling ex-landlords and people from rich families "high class."

There were a few opportunities for me to work in local factories. But my father told me that I should choose further education rather than a factory job. In 1976, my commune informed me that I'd been selected to study in a nursing school in the provincial capital, Hefei. It was a two-year "From the Commune and Back to the Commune" program that was designed to train medics to serve local people. I immediately sent a letter to my family. My father wanted me to take advantage of the opportunity. "Things will change after two years," he told me. "You may not have to return to the countryside." So I enrolled in the school.

Looking back, I think those two years were the happiest in my life. I was in my mid-twenties. However, it was as if I'd begun my childhood all over again. Everyday life was simple and pleasant. The school was for girls only. I can't recall any unpleasant incidents. The teachers liked me because I always got good grades. On Sundays they invited another girl and me—the two Shanghainese—to dinners and outings.

Things didn't turn out as my father had hoped. Because the From the Commune and Back to the Commune policy was still in place when I graduated, I was supposed to return to the village. My father sent me a panicky letter. "Don't go back. Just jump onto a train and return to Shanghai." So the Cultural Revolution taught even my father something! He did something he never could have done before. He rebelled!

I did as my father asked. By 1978, there were very few city students left in the countryside. By one route or another, nearly everyone had returned to Shanghai.

Keeping the Family Together

I asked for "resettlement for physical reasons." There was a long waiting list for physical examinations. While I was waiting, the school telegraphed me. The government had decided to make better use of trained nurses and I'd been assigned to a big prefecture hospital. I was torn into parts. I really wanted to go. After all, what kind of future would I have in Shanghai? Even if I were eligible for "resettlement for physical reasons," which was questionable, the best I could hope for was a job in a neighborhood workshop earning 70 cents a day. Of course, if I went to the prefecture hospital I would never again be able to live in Shanghai with my family.

> After 1977, our family gradually was given back the property that was taken from us during the Cultural Revolution.

My eldest brother was iron firm: "You must stay in Shanghai. A family should always be together. To be with your family is better than anything else." The school sent me five telegrams. I ignored them all.

So I stayed in Shanghai. In 1979, [Chinese leader] Deng Xiaoping let all the "sent-down" students reunite with their families. I returned to the village to get my papers in order. I've never been back since.

After 1977, our family gradually was given back the property that was taken from us during the Cultural Revolution. The tenants who had moved into our house moved out again. Father's original salary was returned to him, and he was compensated for lost income. During the difficult years my eldest brother had made lots of sacrifices for our family. Because he had a university degree he was assigned a job in a provincial factory after he'd served just a short time in the countryside. But he sent most of his salary home. He waited very late to get married.

By 1979, my father was back in his old position. At the time, the government's policy was to encourage older people to step down and make room for their unemployed children. My father could have retired and let me take a position at his factory. But he didn't want to. He was so excited to have his old life back. It was a second chance for him, and he was unable to walk away from it.

I couldn't really condemn him. Anyway, the Bureau of Chemical Industry was good enough to resolve the problem by offering me a job in a small factory that was owned collectively.

This factory had been established under the program of "using state enterprises to support collective factories." Material and human resources from state enterprises were to be used to help small factories in their initial stages of development. Gradually, such support would be withdrawn. These factories were supposed to reduce unemployment levels among those of us who had returned from the countryside. Most of the employees in my factory were like me: "sent-down"—now returned—students.

I worked for a while as a laborer. But, because of my medical training, I was appointed the factory's doctor. Everyone congratulated me. It seemed like a good position. I even went to Shanghai Number Two Medical College for an additional half-year training program. Our factory was doing very well. Everything seemed fine. I got married and had my baby daughter.

I never dreamt I would lose my job.

New Challenges and New Corruption

Whom should I blame for this?

In the late 1980s, a corrupt manager led the factory. He was close to retirement. All he wanted was to line his own pocket before it was too late. He literally sold us out to foreign capitalists by starting a joint venture with a Taiwanese-American businessman. The first thing he and his partner did was to construct a fancy building inside the factory and fence it off as their "joint-venture zone." The manager made a fortune by giving the construction work to those willing to pay the highest bribe. Next, the Taiwanese-American got his cut by dumping outdated poor quality machines on us. Then he disappeared. Our boss got his chance to visit America. So, both partners got what they wanted. They no longer cared whether the joint venture would ever produce anything of value.

Our factory had borrowed foreign currency from the government at the old rate of one US$1 to 5.3 yuan. The debt rose to 10 million yuan at the new exchange rate, which we had no hope of repaying. Our factory had to stop production. The manager said "so long" and retired. What angered us most was that, before he left, he installed a home telephone for "job purposes" and billed the factory. Can you imagine? Even at the last minute he was still trying to grab something for himself.

Six months ago, our factory closed down entirely. We've been given 160 yuan (US$19.25) per month to live on and told to find jobs ourselves. At first, we couldn't believe what was happening. We went to our Bureau to talk to the chief and other officials, hoping they could do something. They recommended we sing three songs: "The Communist Internationale," "Unity is Strength" and "The Field of Hope." They claimed these stirring anthems would give us the spirit we needed.

Well, we got some spirit all right. We organized, and began to frequent the Municipal Economic Planning Committee and the General Workers' Union. We pointed out this is supposed to be a socialist country. We're able-bodied and need work to feed our families. We were desperate. Whenever we saw an official in a corridor or in an office we forced him to listen to us. Finally, the authorities decided they'd had enough. They didn't like us visiting them in groups. So they sent a work team to our factory and ordered us to direct our grievances to them. Every day now, the team just sits there, drinks tea and chats freely with anyone who wants to meet with them. It's no real help but it's a good strategy. We had to stop bothering the bureaucrats.

Yesterday, I went to the factory and discovered there were no funds for unemployment compensation, even though we are supposed to be paid in two days. There's no money to reimburse workers for medical expenses. If you get sick you're on your own.

> "I've tried to get every kind of job. . . . No one wants to hire me. I've given up all hope."

Our newspapers often claim shamelessly that some people got richer after they were laid off because they had the opportunity to pick up better-paid jobs. But not a single person in my factory has a better life now than he or she did before. Since the factory closed down I've tried to get every kind of job. But China doesn't suffer from a labor shortage. Every place I've looked wanted people under 35 years old. I'm a woman in my mid-forties. No one wants to hire me. I've given up all hope.

Rather than bitch about life's unfairness I might as well hang myself. I don't want always to have to compare my situation with people who are better off—especially not with my brothers and sisters. They still have their jobs. Indeed, my second eldest brother is doing very well. He's in real estate and making lots of money. I don't resent the ones who did well. All I want is a job to support my family. I don't expect to be wealthy. My husband's salary is very small. Everything is so expensive today. The average salary used to be 60 yuan a month. Now the lowest basic wage is 600 yuan.

Yesterday I had to pay 375 yuan for my daughter's school fees. I know that if she wants to go to university we'll not be able to pay for it.

> My daughter knows nothing about the Cultural Revolution.

My daughter used to have school lunches. In the past, I could afford this. I thought it was a good way to encourage independence and responsibility. I didn't want her grandparents to wait on her every day. But now she has to come home for lunch.

A Post-Revolutionary Generation

My daughter knows about the changes in our life. She told me: "Mama, I can't compete with my classmates on anything except grades." She is always top in her school. She's my pleasure, hope and everything. She's grown up a lot since I lost my job. When she sees me tired she comes up to me and hammers my back with her fists. "I'll give you a massage," she says.

My daughter knows nothing about the Cultural Revolution. She asks me lots of questions: "Why didn't you go to university?" "Why did people come and take things away from grandpa's home?" "Were they bad people?" It's very difficult for me to share my history with her. It's hard for her to understand. What's the point of bothering her with stories of the past?

When the reforms began I had great hopes. I never expected that things would become worse for ordinary people. I blame our government. Now we're expected to believe that everything about capitalism is good, just as we used to be told that everything about socialism was good. Our government doesn't know how to learn from the West. We copy only the bad things. In the past we were poor, and life wasn't easy. But I never had this feeling of panic all the time, like a heavy rock in my stomach. In the morning, after I've done my chores, I feel lost, not knowing what I should do next.

Let me tell you something. Whenever I cook I put on my doctor's white coat. It's a good use of my profession.

CHRONOLOGY

1949   Mao Zedong and the Chinese Communist Party take control of China after their forces enter the capital, Beijing.

1958–1961   Mao enacts the Great Leap Forward, his attempt to intensify China's industrial development and expand farm production. Millions die from famines that result from the poor production and distribution of food. Mao's reputation suffers.

1961–1964   Economic reformers Deng Xiaoping and Liu Shaoqi reject many of the policies of the Great Leap Forward as Mao's influence continues to wane in China's inner circles.

1965   *Quotations from Chairman Mao Tse-tung*, originally compiled by the People's Liberation Army (PLA), gains official sanction from the Chinese government. Published in a small format and known as the *Little Red Book*, it will become the key text of the Cultural Revolution.

1966   May 16: Having fallen once again under Mao Zedong's control, the Central Committee of the Chinese Communist Party announces the beginning of the Cultural Revolution.

June 1: Mao's "big-character poster" announcing the Cultural Revolution is posted at Beijing University.

June 2: The first unit of Red Guards is formed at

Qinghua University in Beijing and at high schools connected to it. Similar groups quickly take shape throughout the country, and regular coursework at universities and high schools comes to an end.

August: Red Guards begin their campaign to destroy the "Four Olds": old ideas, old culture, old customs, and old habits. Their methods include attacks on schools, temples, and museums.

August 1: Mao pledges to support the Red Guards as the leading edge of the Cultural Revolution.

August 5: Red Guards beat to death Bian Zhongyun, a principal at Beijing Teacher's College. She is the first of hundreds of victims.

August 8: The Central Committee releases its sixteen-point statement of goals for the Cultural Revolution.

August–November: In visits to Beijing, as many as eleven million Red Guards congregate in Tiananmen Square to be recognized by Mao.

October: Deng Xiaoping and Liu Shaoqi are purged from China's inner circle.

1967 January–July: Red Guards expand their influence in Shanghai and other cities, targeting temples and monuments as well as "antirevolutionary" forces.

July: Political leadership in China is placed in the hands of Lin Biao and Mao's wife, Jiang Qing, who publicly support the Cultural Revolution. Mao remains in overall control.

1968 October: Former Mao associate Liu Shaoqi is ousted from the Chinese Communist Party.

December: The "Down to the Countryside" movement begins. Thousands of city dwellers are "sent down" to rural areas for peasant labor and revolutionary re-education.

1969   Universities and high schools begin to reopen and graduates are permitted to take degrees. The gradual process across China takes several years.

1971   Lin Biao, named as Mao's successor, dies in a plane crash.

1972   February: US president Richard Nixon travels to China for visits with Mao Zedong and Premier Zhou Enlai, marking a thaw in US-China relations.

1973   Deng Xiaoping is politically rehabilitated and named vice-premier under Zhou Enlai.

1976   January: Zhou Enlai dies and is replaced as premier by Hua Guofeng in April. The faction headed by Hua and Deng is opposed by the Gang of Four—Mao's wife Jiang Qing and her three principal associates, Wang Hongwen, Zhang Chunqiao, and Yao Wenyuan—who plan to continue elements of the Cultural Revolution.

April: Millions gather in Tiananmen Square to protest the Gang of Four. The protests are violently put down.

September 9: Mao Zedong dies.

October 6: The Gang of Four is arrested under directions from Hua Guofeng. The move is supported by the leadership of the PLA and symbolizes the end of the Cultural Revolution.

1977 Deng Xiaoping, slowly outmaneuvering Hua Guofeng as China's leader, repudiates the Cultural Revolution, allowing public criticism of its events.

1978 Deng introduces a set of economic reforms known as "socialism with Chinese characteristics," setting in motion a process of liberalization that would lead to widespread economic growth.

1981 The Chinese Communist Party passes a resolution blaming the excesses of the Cultural Revolution on Mao Zedong. The Gang of Four is put on trial.

2011 China replaces Japan as the world's second largest economy after the United States.

FOR FURTHER READING

Books

Barbara Barnouin and Yu Changgen, *Ten Years of Turbulence: The Chinese Cultural Revolution*. London: Kegan Paul International, 1993.

Gordon A. Bennett and Ronald N. Montaperto, *Red Guard: The Political Biography of Dai Hsiao-ai*. Garden City, NY: Doubleday, 1971.

Timothy Cheek, *Mao Zedong and China's Revolutions: A Brief History with Documents*. Boston: Bedford/St. Martins, 2002.

Nien Cheng, *Life and Death in Shanghai*. London: Grafton Books, 1986.

Paul Clark, *The Chinese Cultural Revolution: A History*. New York: Cambridge University Press, 2008.

Han Dongping, *The Unknown Cultural Revolution*. New York: Monthly Review Press, 2008.

John Fairbank, *The Great Chinese Revolution 1800–1985*. New York: Harper and Row, 1986.

Lin Jing, *The Red Guards' Path to Violence*. New York: Praeger, 1991.

William A. Joseph, et al. eds., *New Perspectives on the Cultural Revolution*. Cambridge, MA: Council on East Asian Studies, 1991.

Stanley Karnow, *Mao and China: A Legacy of Turmoil*. New York: Penguin, 1990.

Ziping Luo, *A Generation Lost: China Under the Cultural Revolution*. New York: H. Holt, 1990.

Harrison E. Salisbury, *The New Emperors: China in the Era of Mao and Deng*. New York: Little, Brown, 1992.

Orville Schell, *To Get Rich Is Glorious*. New York: Pantheon, 1985.

David Scott, *China Stands Up: The PRC and the International System*. London: Routledge, 2007.

Edgar Snow, *The Long Revolution*. New York: Random House, 1972.

Jonathan D. Spence, *The Gate of Heavenly Peace: The Chinese and Their Revolution, 1895–1980*. New York: Viking, 1981.

Anne F. Thurston, *Enemies of the People: The Ordeal of the Intellectuals in China's Great Cultural Revolution*. New York: Knopf, 1987.

Chihua Wen, *The Red Mirror: Children of China's Cultural Revolution*. Boulder: Westview Press, 1995.

Jan Wong, *Red China Blues: My Long March from Mao to Now*. New York: Bantam Books, 1996.

Jiaqi Yan and Gao Gao, *Turbulent Decade: A History of the Cultural Revolution*. Honolulu: University of Hawaii Press, 1991.

Periodicals

Phil Baty, "The Long March," *Times* (London), October 29, 2009.

Chris Campling, "Mao, Nixon, and the Ping-pong Breakthrough," *Sunday Times* (London), June 24, 2008.

David Challenger, "In His Hometown, Mao a Source of Pride," *CNN World*, September 13, 2009.

Oriana Fallaci, "Deng, Cleaning Up Mao's 'Feudal Mistakes,'" *Washington Post*, August 31, 1980.

Edward A. Gargan, "Witness to Mao's Crimes," *New York Times*, June 30, 1996.

Frida Knight, "Eyewitness of the Cultural Revolution," *China Now*, no. 139, December 1991.

Joel Kotkin, "Red Guards New Revolt as Capitalists," *Los Angeles Times*, June 12, 1988.

Josh Kurlantzick, "China's Repressed Memory of the Cultural Revolution: Silent Revolution," *New Republic Online*, September 18, 2006.

Andreas Lorenz, "The Chinese Cultural Revolution: Remembering Mao's Victims," *Spiegel Online*, May 15, 2007.

Linda McIntosh, "Memoir Recount's China's Cultural Revolution," *San Diego Union Tribune*, June 5, 2005.

Time, "The Red Guards: Today, China; Tomorrow, the World," September 23, 1966.

Kenneth Walker, "Revisiting China's Cultural Revolution: A Review Article," *Journal of the Royal Asiatic Society of Britain and Ireland*, Third Series, no. 18, 2008.

Ye Yonglie, "China's 'Textbook Problem'," *Danwei*, May 16, 2006.

Websites

China 1900–1976 (www.historylearningsite.co.uk/china_1900_to_1976.htm). This is a website from Great Britain providing summaries on major subjects in recent Chinese history such as the Cultural Revolution, as well as brief biographies of important figures. Each article provides links to related topics.

Discovering China: The Cultural Revolution (http://library.thinkquest.org/26469/cultural-revolution). This website provides articles designed for students on various topics related to the Cultural Revolution. The articles are accompanied by photographs or other illustrations.

Mao's China (www.casahistoria.net/mao_china.htm). This is part of a website on modern history designed for students. It provides links to articles and other websites that touch on features of the Cultural Revolution such as art and literature or propaganda.

Virtual Museum of the Cultural Revolution (www.cnd.org/cr). This website provides lists of various sources on the Cultural Revolution, ranging from personal accounts to official documents.

INDEX

M